The American Indian Reader

• History

By Rupert Costo

The Indian Historian Press, Inc.

American Indian Educational Publishers
San Francisco, Calif.

This series in educational perspectives
is published with the aid of a grant
from The Ford Foundation

The American Indian Reader:

HISTORY

Book Four of a series
in educational perspectives

Jeannette Henry, Editor

Copyright 1974 by
The Indian Historian Press, Inc.
All Rights Reserved
Printed in the United States of America
Library of Congress Catalog Card No. 72-86875
ISBN No. 0-913436-23-2

Contents

Introduction

Before contact with the Europeans, the history of the American Indian was passed down orally from generation to generation. Each tribe, in its own language, possessed its history as part of a venerated body of literature told again and again in the form of epic chronology, religious observance, and legendary chant.

Only the beginnings of a written language had begun to appear in tribes of Central and South America, and among some of the native people of North America. Evidences of such writing were maliciously destroyed by Spanish adventurers. Thus, the great body of a magnificent human story has largely been lost. It exists only in the annals remaining to some tribes in the form of song and observance. Other evidences of ancient native history have been painstakingly put together by anthropologists from physical remains gathered by archaeologists. But the great human epic of the native as he lived in the Western Hemisphere before white contact could be reconstructed only with the greatest difficulty.

One would think, that following the arrival of the Europeans, and access to a universal form of writing, that the native history could have been put down for future generations to learn. But this is not so. The foreign colonizer and adventurer preferred to ignore the native history as it influenced and often determined the destiny of these United States. To this day, even the work of the scholars in piecing together the native's own ancient history has not found its way into the textbooks except in the form of a specialized discipline which is the province of scholars in anthropology.

What of the native history as it unfolded after European contact? This certainly could have been done. The evidence is available. But there is no written history *of the American Indian*. There are only histories of the white man in his relations with the native. Scholars generally agree that their treatment of the Native American, as written history, is from the "outside," largely as it has affected the history of the dominant society. Such a history of the American Indian, either before white contact, or after contact, remains to be written. It is a strange commentary, that before being completely over-run by white conquest, the Indian had and held fast his history as something to be revered and respected. Today, with the great advantage of a universal writing tool, even most young Indians have no knowledge of their human story, either before or after the strangers came. The dominant society has tilted and twisted history in such a way as to serve its own best interests.

Even the chronology of American history, taught to school children, is awry. The date "1492" is taught as the beginning of American history. The first and vastly more important entries into the Western Hemisphere through the North American continent are hidden. In treating of their Europeanized history, the point is missed. It is not the year 1492 that is historically significant. After all, the landing of Christopher Columbus was a fortuitous event, a gigantic historic mistake, as was his naming of the natives as "Indians" a gross error. But it is the year 1494 that is of historic significance. It was then that some five hundred Indians were rounded up like animals and trundled off to Spain to be sold into slavery. The great conflict between the corrupt western monarchies and the native civilizations was now well under way. It would not end for four hundred years, and even at that early date the natives had begun to resist.

A massive re-write of American history is long overdue.

* * * * * *

The *American Indian Reader: History* is a small beginning in providing a body of literature dealing with the history of the American Indian. We do not hold with the concept that such a history is being "told from the Indian point of view." We are attempting to relate the truth in history, as well as to uncover the long hidden facts. Every society to date has educated its young according to the best interests of its dominant class. Perhaps this can change, and humanity be made to see itself face to face without fear and in spite of the pangs of conscience.

The contents of this book are both original, and from the pages of The Indian Historian, the official quarterly periodical of The American Indian Historical Society.

All articles in this Reader are authored by Rupert Costo, except for the paper on "Indian Allotments Preceding the Dawes Act," by Paul W. Gates.

Part I

Before the Invasion

THERE IS A COMMON misconception that history must be presented in written form, by academicians, in order to be worthy of serious consideration. It is seldom recalled that the art of writing as it is known today is only a small time-particle in the story of man. Besides, other systems of writing have existed in ancient times, which science has not yet deciphered. Still another aspect is that the act of writing does not eliminate bias, and more often misinterprets the facts of history.

The American Indian has a strong tradition of oral history. The facts of "life before the invasion" are generally borne out by anthropologists and archaeological evidence, and the conclusions drawn here may be substantiated in a number of ways through their scientific works, in case one doubts the veracity of the native himself.

If "invasion" is accepted as defining "the taking of land by armed force," then it would only partly describe the whole process by which foreigners took the Western Hemisphere from its original owners. Webster has this other definition of the word: "The penetration and gradual occupation of an area by a population group of different socio-economic status or racial or cultural origins than its original inhabitants." The Western Hemisphere was taken not only by armed force. It was invaded by encroachment, intrusion, infiltration, and infringement of natural rights observed for thousands of years by the natives.

1

Thus was the eastern seaboard of the North American continent taken by invasion through the most insidious means. Foreign occupation was justified in the hearts and in the laws of the invaders because they refused to recognize the natives as human beings. Genocide and extermination walked hand in hand with illegal penetration of the land. The first and most deadly result of the invasion was the loss of the native's culture and language, including much of his oral history. Still did the native endure, and endures today. The culture has changed. Much of it has been irretrievably lost. Many languages remain, even though in altered form, having met the same fate as the culture and the land. In some tribes the language is as strong as it ever was, and this is true, for example, of the Navajo Indian Nation, the Pueblos, and the Apaches. In a few tribes and among a few people, the language is all that survives, as in the case of a branch of the Mohawks.

But the history of the American Indian lives on. Information such as the place, the date, or the ways in which a certain tribe came to a specific region is no longer available except in the most general terms. Nor, when there was conflict among the tribes, is there information as to where and when and by what means a certain battle took place. On the contrary, the western civilization historians give a blow-by-blow account of the gory details of their wars. In the first place, our "conflicts" were resolved in traditional humane ways. In the west, around the region known now as California, differences were usually settled by mock battles, one person being chosen to represent his tribe in the mock battle against the other tribe which had also chosen one representative warrior. In the eastern part of the country, some tribes took captives, and after a period of menial work, were generally adopted into the tribe. These are only two, isolated, examples. The facts are buried in the thousands upon thousands of years during which we lived here, worked here, bore our children here, and built our lives in this our native land.

The native peoples had developed their own civilization during those thousands of years before the European invasion. Estimates vary as to how many years they had occupied the two continents of the hemisphere, from not less than 10,000 years before Christ, to as much as 40,000 years.

"Where did they come from?" is the question usually asked as the student begins his study of American Indian his-

2

tory. Most anthropologists say that the Indian did not originate in the Western Hemisphere. They point to a lack of evidence of any prior biological form of life, from which man could have evolved here. They hold to the theory that man first entered North America from Asia, by way of the Bering Isthmus, the geological aspects of the land at that time being vastly different than they are today, and the isthmus forming a virtual "land bridge" from Asia to North America. But there is scientific evidence now coming to light which may prove that the Indians did indeed originate a new race of people here at some time in the most distant past. There are many Indians who themselves believe that they have been here "forever." On the other hand, there is strong evidence, as well as tradition and belief on the part of the Indian people, that many tribes and groups of families came "from the north," or "from the sea," or from "the south." One is dealing, in this discussion, with the history of man himself, and with the history of a people whose life in the Western Hemisphere spans thousands upon thousands of years. The question of original entry, migrations from one area to another, and the gradual historic settlement of the tribes and nations upon one area or another, is a matter for a separate volume, and it cannot be pursued here. Suffice it to say, that the Native American has been in this hemisphere long enough to claim ownership, long enough to develop his own civilization, and long enough to be recognized as the discoverers, explorers, and settlers of this land.

Another question which has been of equal importance with the question of origins is the matter of demography, or population. Historians and anthropologists have produced such varying figures in guessing the numbers of natives living here prior to the invasion, that at times their estimates seem ludicrous in the light of the Indian's knowledge of the facts. Some anthropologists have tidily counted the lodges, or dwellings of a certain tribe or settlement, then estimated the average number of people presumed to have occupied each dwelling, then multiplied this number by the number of dwellings, and have then come up with an uneducated guess. The population of North America, therefore, has been variously estimated by the scholars at 750,000 down to 450,000 for the entire continent. Through the years, however, the estimate has crept up to one million natives living here before white contact. Now, the estimate is being marked up appreciably. It's time that the facts, as known to the Indians themselves, be taken into account. In the California region alone, which is now artificially bounded by the states of Arizona, Nevada, and Oregon, as well as by Mexico and Lower California, the *Indian country* contained parts of western Arizona, Northern Mexico, northern Lower California, western Nevada, and southern Oregon. In this area there were not less than one million natives prior to white contact. If the word of the native be not taken seriously, witness the thousands upon thousands of burial sites, cemeteries, and gravesites now coming to light by archaeological excavation. It has been stated that one can't dig very far into any area of California or Arizona without finding evidence that the natives lived here, hunted here, fished here, or buried their dead here. A current count of such archaeological sites in Arizona alone comes up with a figure of approximately 14,000 sites. A population count cannot be made on the basis of such sites, certainly. But this fact, coupled with the knowledge of the natives, gives credence to the native claim of a population figure vastly larger than the estimates of anthropologists, even those who assume themselves to be experts in demography.

In Peru, the estimate of population varies from thirty million to sixty million. In the east, the population of the Iroquois is estimated at anywhere from 50,000 to 75,000. It seems perfectly logical to this writer, himself a Cahuilla Indian of southern California, member of a numerous clan, a numerous tribe, and a numerous nation of original Americans, that the figure of four million inhabiting the North American continent is not too large a number.

Why then does the United States Government, in its official publications and its propaganda through the Bureau of Indian Affairs, place the estimated population figure so low? The answer is simple. The basic reason is the frightening decline of the Indian population following white contact. Many tribes disappeared completely. Population estimes by the United States have varied, from time to time, following the opening of the 18th century, of 400,000 to a maximum of 600,000. In California, where there were approximately one million natives, there was counted in 1854, a population of not more than 18,000. This was after the gold rush, when Indians were exterminated in masses, and by various means. But even if an anthropological estimate of about 150,000 (Kroeber) is accepted, such a decline is little short of murder, and certainly can be considered woll within the definition of genocide. How did the people die? First of all, by destruction of their economy and the resultant famine. Secondly, by way of the white man's diseases such as syphillis, gonorrhea, diphtheria, influenza, pneumonia, and smallpox. The purity of life in the natural state provided no immunity to such diseases, and the people died. Genocide by way of shooting, giving the people food which was laced with arsenic, or beating them to death, was another cause of population decline. It is really not too difficult to reconstruct the population, the tribes, and the way of life of the native in the California region just prior to white contact. The Spanish missionaries came in the latter half of the 18th century in this area. Thus, the picture of the natives before the invasion becomes clear and the outrages committed against them become more pernicious in the eyes of humanity the world over.

Over-generalization and simplification of the native culture, languages, economy, and traditions of the Indian before the invasion are the two great dangers in historic interpretation. Various stages of civilization existed, from the complex societies of Central America and South America, to the less complex societies of California and other parts of the west. There were great cities in Peru, magnificent temples in Mexico, definite social classes in many regions. The Hopewell and Adena cultures in the southern and midwestern parts of the United States, with their splendid temples, stockaded towns, and complex social structure existed side by side with societies having extensive land holdings where they had their hunting and fishing and harvesting areas well established, moving from place to place with the seasons. Thus, over-generalization and an attempt to simplify native history before white contact, will surely lead the student or historian down a blind alley, with the dangers of error and misinterpretation dogging his every footstep. The textbooks are filled with these two enemies of historic fact.

There are two elements in dealing with the history of the Indian that are critical in the development of understanding. One is the element of time. The historian, attempting to squeeze the native into a single history of the United States, as an example, generalizes the native society to such a degree that there can be no consideration of a dynamic interpretation of that society. The years bring changes; society changes; man changes; history is not static. Having wrecked our culture and nearly destroyed our oral history, therefore, our time element in considering the period before the invasion, is forced to deal merely with hundreds of years instead of tens of thousands. We leave it to the scholars in anthropology and archaeology to reconstruct the remnants of our lives during the millenia in which we lived here. The second element is the sense of accumulated facts which makes it possible to reach certain inescapable conclusions.

It is a fact, substantiated by the accumulation of information both by the native historian and the scientist, that the native peoples owned the entire Western Hemisphere. Discovery and aboriginal settlement was as complete for that stage of history as it could be. There was no "undiscovered land" at the time of the European invasion. All the land, the waters and streams, the mountains and valleys, had been discovered by the native, were known by the native, were utilized and assigned by ancentral tribal right. Assignment was by tribal right, by joint use understandings or agreements, or by centuries of occupancy. Natural catastrophies or food failures caused tribes to move into other areas. The fantasy of an "undiscovered wilderness" is a dream of the ignorant, and a crutch for the historian who is attempting to justify the ignominious actions of the invaders.

The concept of "vacant land" as propounded by the American historian Frederick Jackson Turner, is just such a fantasy, and is an attempt to lend credence to the idea that the white man "tamed" the American wilderness. The ideology upon which this theory is founded is that if land was indeed "vacant," then the movement of westward expansion and the opening of the western "frontier" was just, honorable, and even admirable. That this was not the truth, is now being accepted by responsible historians. The civilization of the American Indian before the invasion was of an entirely different order than any in existence at that time anywhere in the world.

The key to understanding any society lies in its economy. How people make their living, to what degree their arts and inventions have been developed, their relationship to the land, their uses of the land, and the nature of their labors and laboring force . . . all these are factors influencing their culture, tradition, arts, and religions. The extent to which ancient society in the Americas had become a complex economy before European contact, is seen in their development of money as a method of exchange of goods. In this case, too, generalization is dangerous. But it is to be remembered that the use of money comes only after an excess of goods has been created. Thus, this type of economy is seen as developing beyond the bounds of mere barter or exchange of one article for another. In some areas indeed (the Iroquois as one example), the economy had developed to such a degree that a form of money had evolved. The use of wampum in this respect is well known, and we need not at this point enter into a discussion of other uses of wampum for purposes of this survey. In the northwest as well, a form of money had evolved. In other areas, such as those in the far west, the method of exchange of goods by barter was in general use, although the use of dentalium as a form of money had already begun. People needed certain pottery. They exchanged other goods with various tribes that had articles they needed. Thus, the cinnabar quarry at San Jose, California, became famous as a source of highly-prized vermillion, used in religious observances, and as a decorative paint. The people came from as far away as Vancouver, B.C. to trade for the vermillion. A similar situation existed at Pipestone, where the great mines may be seen even today. The people came from areas miles away to obtain the sacred pipestone, with the permission of the Sioux. Beautiful California-made baskets have been found in New Mexico; while the extraordinary pottery of the Pueblos have been found in California. Great trails and highways existed, along which the natives traveled in their quest for trade. Indeed trade was general, and a detailed analysis of its development can be read in *Contributions and Achievements of the American Indian.*

The native peoples are often described as "nomads," wandering from area to area "in search of food." This brings up a picture of an aimless and wandering people without roots anywhere in the land, drifting from land area to land area like any herd of animals. This idea is also advanced because of the necessity to avoid recognition of actual ownership of the land before the invasion. First of all, a nomadic people are not necessarily "wanderers," without aim and a home base. Second, this over-generalization places the people in the position of being without a formal society, without definite government, subject to the perils of being overrun by any larger and better organized group. It is forgotten or if it is remembered, it is treated as an isolated phenomenon, that a great many of the

7

tribes knew and practiced farming. There were great farming areas in the southwest, and in the eastern United States. Corn was one of the first crops. Other cultivated plants included the sunflower, ragweed, pigweed, cotton, and peanuts. Fully fifty percent of the plants used in the world today have come from the native peoples of the Western Hemisphere. These are domesticated plants that must be planted, tended, the soil cared for in order not to exhaust it, so that the greatest yield may be harvested and to insure better and improved varieties. The Incas developed an extraordinary textile industry, still one of marvels of world economic and artistic history. The native people built unique irrigation plants, as witness the underground irrigation plant at Palm Springs, California. One need only point to the society developed by the peace-loving Pueblo people to know that this was a great and rewarding civilization. The Pueblo irrigation canals near the ancient city of Los Muertos, watered as much as 200,000 acres of their land.

The Indian people mined copper, and their knowledge and use of minerology is well known and fully substantiated. Apartment houses built of stone, the first in North America to be recognizably known as this type of multi-family dwelling, testifies to the remarkable nature of the Pueblo civilization. Besides their irrigation ditches, which they carefully tended, the Pueblo people had a stable economy, with a highly respected form of government, and a complex system of religion that tied them to the land and showed values of human relationships that are still the envy of western civilization.

In Yucatan, cement roads were built, thousands of years before a Scottish engineer invented the macadam (or broken rock) road surface. Their roads stretched mile after mile, embracing in ribbon-like character, the fields and forests and cities of their land. The tar beds at La Brea, California, testify to their knowledge and use of asphaltum as a binding agent.

Trade existed, and not only within the bounds of just a part of the North American continent, now known as the United States. There was international trade, a high-sounding designation beloved by the politically orientated nations of today. Pottery and textiles came from the Mayas; emeralds and pearls from Colombia; turquoise from New Mexico; cacao from southern Central America; baskets from California as well as the highly-prized abalone shell. The fact that the natives knew only the boundaries of people-to-people is testified to by the great

8

fairs held in Siberia, to which the Eskimos of Alaska traveled every year. Here they exchanged and traded for skins, pots, certain foods. Thus was commerce and trade a normal part of the economy, varying in character from simple barter, to trade by exchange considered in quantities of articles suitable for other quantities of articles, to the use of money as a medium of exchange. Contrary to general opinion, most of this commerce was carried on by sea, not overland. Boats traveling from the southernmost tip of South America traversed and navigated the perilous ocean to trade with tribes of the north. From the skinboats of the Eskimos in Alaska, to the great canoes of the Yuroks in northern California, on to the unique canoe of the Chumash near Santa Barbara, California, and the boats of the South American countries bordering on the Pacific Ocean, these sea-going vessels astounded the first Europeans who encountered them, and became models for many types of watercraft known today.

The great apartment houses of the Pueblos were not the only form of dwelling certainly, developed by the Native Americans. Houses varied from the skin-covered tipis of the plains people, to the remarkable log houses of the Yuroks in the northwest, to the longhouses of the Iroquois; (they are known even today as "People of the Longhouse"). Evidences of the Hopewell and Adena log houses of mid-America exist. They were circular in shape, made of posts lashed together. The Iroquois dwellings were made of stout poles, ten feet high, set vertically at every four feet. Rafters, bent into a pointed arch, were lashed together to the top of the poles. The roof was covered with slabs of elm bark. These longhouses were usually fifty to one hundred feet long and twenty feet wide. The dwellings built by many California tribes were of poles forming a basic foundation, covered with brush, and then covered with earth. The Navajo hogans have been described often, and are still being used as the best form of dwelling in that arid land, although modified today to some extent. Indeed the culture evidenced by the types of dwellings used by the natives persisted well into the 18th Century.

The tribes knew their boundaries, and trespass was good cause for conflict. The Mohawks, as one example, lived in upper New York State and on the far side of the St. Lawrence river in Canada. The Blackfeet lived both in Canada and the United States. Certain tribes at the southernmost edge of California were and are today blood relatives of those living in northern Mexico. The Cherokees had a hunting range that covered the Appalachian Highlands in North and South Carolina, areas in Northern Alabama, the Cumberland Plateau in Tennessee, west to Muscle Shoals, and north to the Ohio, and extended into Virginia, West Virginia and Kentucky.

Before the invasion, the Indians used tools, from varying degrees of simplicity to the considerable sophistication of the Central American peoples. Tools were made of flint and bone or wood. Labor was fully utilized, and the excellence of the spears and knives of the American Indian are even today recognized. Rope was made of vegetable fibers, sea vegetation, and bark. Evidence of complex pulleys still exist in the southwest, and ladders were widely used by the people of the Southwest.

The Native Americans had developed their own calendric systems, varying from the Maya system to that of the Cherokees of the southern United States. The Mayas also developed their mathematics to such a degree that their invention of the zero cannot be taken from them, in recognition of their high culture and civilization. They knew the zero at least 700 years before the birth of Christ. While the great culture of the Indians of the southern continent is generally recognized, although grudgingly in many cases, it is nevertheless said that this culture was not seen in North America, thereby misrepresenting the people of the northern continent as mere "savages."

With all the evidence pointing to national and international trade, is it possible for anyone to believe that the works of the people of the southern continent were unknown to those of the north? That would be a foolish supposition, yet it is either stated or implied in many history books and most particularly in the textbooks used by children in public-supported schools.

The basic social system was the family. From the family came the clan, and from the clan the tribe was developed. A number of tribal entities related by origin or association, made up the Nation. Yet even this relatively simple description cannot be applied to the whole society. The family is the basis for any social system in ancient life. Combinations of families might come about because of the need to consolidate varying forces in the face of natural disasters, the lack of food, and availability of productive land. Tribes might be composed of previously unrelated peoples, cooperating and then consolidating because of the same reasons. But these processes took thousands and

10

at the least hundreds of years, and the overview of development of any tribal society must be accomplished on a tribal basis. Now that some tribes are writing their own histories, it is to be hoped that much of this information will be available.

Native governments also varied in type and structure. These too must be studied by tribal group. It is sufficient to note that a considerable variety of tribal governments existed. Of particular interest is the growth of a system of confederation between the tribes and nations. Most generally known is the Iroquois Confederacy, which was comprised of the Mohawk, Oneida, Onondaga, Cayuga and Seneca. Later, after white contact, the Tuscaroras joined the Confederacy, for their protection and survival. Each tribe had independent political existence, the confederacy uniting on issues of mutual interest. Known also as the Five Nations, this confederation was established long before the Europeans landed at Plymouth Rock, and continued for some hundreds of years until conflicts between the whites (French-English-American) divided their loyalties and broke apart their unity. They called themselves, in their own tongues, "people of the entended lodge."

Other organizational formations of the various tribal entities existed in North America. Some of these, sometimes called "alliances" rather than strictly confederacies, were: the Chippewa, Ottawa, and Potawatomie; the Seven Council Fires of the Dakotas; and the Powhaton Confederacy, which allied the tribes of Virginia and Maryland. The Delaware Confederacy occupied the entire basin of the Delaware river in eastern Pennsylvania and southeast New York, together with most of New Jersey and Delaware. Among themselves they were called the Leni Lenape. So far as is known, the great tribes in this confederacy were known as the Minsee, Unami, and Unalachtigo; but these were really the three divisions of the Delawares, in which also some smaller tribes living in New Jersey joined. The democracy practiced by these tribes became a model for the young United States when they began to form a confederation of their own. It was Benjamin Franklin who said, with some degree of envy, how amazing it was that a group of "savages" like the Iroquois, had found it possible to create a democratic government such as the Five Nations Confederacy, while the civilized American colonies found so much difficulty in forming a united confederation of their own.

The unique and complex system of government developed

by the Iroquois, the Cherokees, the Delawares and most of the tribes of the eastern seaboard varied from that of other tribes in the midwest, or the west, and certainly from the form of government developed by the Maya or Inca of the southern continent. But the over-riding principle and philosophy of government these "savages" developed, was based on the much touted democratic theory of "consent of the governed," which became a propaganda phrase among the European invaders.

The origin of that philosophy belongs to the Iroquois, although it existed in various other forms among other tribal groups of the North American continent. The founding of this philosophy, the creation of government and its functions as a result of it, and the initiating of a new and humane society based on this philosophy, belongs to the Iroquois and to them alone.

The Indians had developed, along with their various types of civilization, their own systems of crime and justice. This too varied from tribe to tribe. But it can be said that the basis for meting out justice was that of remuneration, unlike that of the western European nations, which demanded punishment for the sake of punishment.

The breadth of creative intelligence, and the level of a humane philosophy can best be seen in the arts of a people. The rock art of the Indian is well known. So too are his paintings on skin. His pottery still are examples of world-recognized artistry. The temples, tribal edifices and other buildings con structed both in certain areas of North America and in Central and South America are examples of man at his height of artistic accomplishment. The artist was recognized, respected, revered. And the relationship between the people and their artists was close and filled with delight for both. The museums are filled with examples of the art of the native, gathered from all parts of the Western Hemisphere. It is truly amazing that a good deal of their arts, particularly in design, are still unknown. As one example, the attire of the northwest tribes brought surprise to a group in the nation's capitol recently, when shown the Hoopa dress of the women. Most people believe that the design work of the Plains Indians is all that exists of Indian artistry and ingenuity.

After the early Spanish conquistadores' description of the natives as "heathens," it must have come as quite a shock to the western civilized world, to learn that the Natives were highly religious people, worshipping their god, observing the rules and rituals of their religion, and founding their beliefs and religious traditions on their relationship with "Mother Earth," the sun, the sky, the moon and the stars. Nature was all powerful. They believed it. They practiced their beliefs. And who is to say that they were wrong, considering the great variety of beliefs and religions the world has known. It was perhaps this body of beliefs which was their final undoing. Because they were certain that others would keep their word, just as they kept theirs; that others would not despoil the land, just as they revered it; and that others would not treat the land like any other commodity, buying and selling it, just as they had refused to buy and sell their land through the years immemorial that they had lived in this place.

Part II

The Barbarians

THERE IS LITTLE doubt that we had foreign visitors from time to time, during the thousands of years our people lived in these two continents. Many stories and some theories exist about the strangers who landed on our shores, some on the eastern seaboard, others in the southern continent, still others along the southern shores made accessible by the Gulf of Mexico. Some theories are spun by storytellers. Others are the result of anthropological and historical studies, attempting to reconstruct the history of those who peopled the Western Hemisphere.

There are some theories advanced by people who want to prove a point. As one example, in the book by Jennings Wise (*Red Men in the New World Drama*, Vine Deloria, Jr., editor), a historic "point" has been attempted. Mr. Wise was an ardent Presbyterian who attempted to explain that Norwegians and Scandinavians came to North America and settled here for a time, some traveling to the south. He states that evidences of certain forms of a higher culture are the results of these European influences. Other theories of this type have been propounded from time to time, and the conscious or unconscious purpose of such ideas is to deprive the native of his inventions, his innovations, and his vast contributions to the world.

Supposedly, the Native American didn't have the brains, the character, or the intelligence, to develop a high culture.

14

We deny such claims, and oppose such inferences. Our own history, as revealed in our legendry, mythology, and oral literature, is more to be believed than the work of some scholars, so-called "experts" in native history. Our oral history does indeed speak of the visits of strangers through the millenia. These visits were short-lived. For one reason or another, the strangers went away. What remained, following their departure, is enclosed in our history. We are not a party to the controversy among scholars, of "diffusion versus independent invention." Further scientific investigation will prove that the native did produce innovations and that he exercised a great inventive human mind. It will also prove that all the people of the earth, for long thousands of years, borrowed ideas as well as techniques. Where was the beginning? Who did it first? These are questions which we will leave to the professional scientific earthworm, knowing very well that once a beginning is discovered, the search will start again, only to end in yet another beginning, yet another date.

The ancient memory and oral history does not deal in the exact dates of the western calendric system. That system, for one thing, is not as exact as the one invented by the ancient Mayas. But the history is there in the oral literature, and is well worthy of reference.

The native lived in a land rich with vegetation, game, fish, streams and forests. In the words of Garanpela, when he spoke to the governor of Canadian Quebec in 1684: "We are born free. We may go where we please, and carry with us whom we please, and buy and sell what we please." The one thing the native did not sell, however, was his land. But the sense and the actuality of freedom with responsibility was there. When the foreigners came, then, it was with great wonder we learned of their concept of land and its uses. It was also with wonder that we viewed their appearance, their modes and manners, their way of life, and their habits of husbandry (such as they were).

They were a strange looking sort. We marvelled how their bodies could breathe, they were so tied up and bound with various garments. Their feet were sheathed in leathers. Underneath were more garments. Their bodies were draped with all kinds of strange leggings, blouses, and frills. Wide brimmed hats bestrode their heads, so that the sun and the air could not brush their brows. They were very pale, so it was clear

15

to us that they were a sickly lot. They were sadly neglected, too. The men had allowed the hair to grow all over their faces, so that one had no idea of what they really looked like under all that foliage. Coming close to them, their bodies stank. Obviously they bathed but seldom, and in time we discovered that bathing was not in their habitual manner of living, and then they had to have special equipment and accoutrements. We surprised some of them in this ritual, and to our great wonder, we found them stuck in a wooden tub, their feet dangling outside, water being warmed over a fire by their women, who waited on them hand and foot, and rubbing themselves all over with some kind of foul-smelling stuff which they called "soap." In contrast, we bathed daily in the cool, clear waters of the purest streams. We used a soap made of the vegetation that grew on our land, invented by our forefathers, and used through the centuries by the native people. The smell of our bodies was as the scent of the woods, and we were proud of a good body in perfect health.

It is not surprising, therefore, that when the foreigners first came in our sight, our people surrounded them, wondering and marvelling at these strange beings. We thought they were from another place in the universe, and many of us could not believe they were human beings. Curiosity overwhelming some of the people, they felt of the clothing, touched the hands and the faces of these people, reassuring themselves that indeed they were persons, like the native people. In some cases, our people thought they were gods, come from the heavens to be with us for a time and then leave for their celestial homes. In other cases, the people viewed these visitors with fear and alarm, sensing danger in the sudden appearance of such beings.

In the beginning, we met these people with friendly hospitality and loving kindness. The elders explained that probably we appeared just as "strange" to the visitors as they appeared to us, and that the principles of hospitality should prevail, impelling us to cease exhibiting such curiosity as would make the newcomers uneasy.

Thus, seeing their pale and haggard faces when we first met them on the eastern seaboard, the first thing we did was to feed them, help them find shelters for they had no houses and were strangers in our land, and bring them corn and fruits, berries, squashes, and game of various kinds.

Our people in other parts of North America had experiences

of the same kind, generally. In California, when the soldiers and priests came (much later than they arrived in the east), they were all gussied up in yards of clothing. The men had metal on their breasts, and they used plumes of a strange type, which floated from their hats. The long dark cassocks of men whom we later came to know as priests frightened many of our people, they looked so ominous and forbidding. The first thing these people did was to throw themselves upon the ground, uttering strange noises in their strange language. Then they turned to those of us who had come to stare open-mouthed at these strange creatures, and by motions and shoving, we too were forced to kneel upon the ground, for no reason that we could divine. Then one of the strangers produced a long white paper, from which he made noises in his strange language. We had no idea of the meaning of this kind of a performance. But we were glad to oblige them, if it made them happy. Later, we were to find out that with that paper, and in those strange noises of their strange language, they had enslaved our people. This was the proclamation of their head man in a faraway land, whom they called "king." He and they had declared our land to be theirs alone, and constituted it an outpost of the Spanish crown. We found this out later, much later. What happened to us is engraved upon the racial memory. We put the records of these happenings in the hands of our elders, those who kept the history, and thenceforward they were related every time the occasion arose when the history was told, and when the young were taught by the grandmothers and grandfathers. However, the foreigners with their pale and sickly faces kept records in their own way. Our elders were killed; our culture was destroyed; and much of our spoken history and literature was lost. But there are still those of us remaining even today, who know the history, and together with the records of the palefaces we can reconstruct the whole miserable story, weeding out the truth from the falsehoods, even as we carefully weeded out a certain excess of young trees from the forests so that the others might grow strong and tall.

In time, these foreigners came to be called, in our many languages and dialects, by words meaning (in the style of today) *Barbarians*.

Let us analyze the word *Barbarian*. According to a respectable, Anglo, accepted definition, the word means, first: "of or

17

relating to a land, culture, or people alien and usually believed to be inferior to one's own." True, the first barbarians who came to us didn't know how to hunt, dressed abominably and in poor fashion for life in our land, and had practices which were below the dignity of man. Such as burning people at the stake because their opinions differed from theirs; forcing people to pray whether they wanted to or not; forcing people to pray in the way prescribed by a certain hierarchy; and not even being aware of the existence of corn or how to plant it. Another definition is: "lacking refinement, gentleness, learning, artistic or literary culture; marked by a tendency toward brutality, violence, or lawlessness." Indeed the barbarians lacked "refinement." Their manners were atrocious; they were not hospitable; they knew nothing of the habits of a clean body; they clutched a man's hand in greeting, pumping it up and down in a most ugly manner, instead of gracefully bending the head or raising the hand in greeting. They told lies, as we know, having caught them at it all through our unfortunate history with them.

As to "gentleness," most of them were abrupt, sharp of tongue, loud of voice, and behind the courtly manner of some few of them, they were mean and dangerous. If they had any "learning," it was beyond our means of discovering it, for they knew nothing about us and nothing of our country nor our ways of life. They couldn't even speak our language, while we, on the other hand, although there were many tribes with different languages in our country, always managed to converse one with another. This was done either through many of our people learning to understand by hearing, the language of another tribe, or using our fine sign language. The foreigners were adrift in their ignorance of our tongues. It is a fact, that we learned to speak their language, whether French, English or Dutch, long before they learned ours. There were more Indians who interpreted English into Indian, than there were English who interpreted Indian into English. In many parts of our country, there were natives who spoke three languages: Indian, Spanish, and English; or Indian, French and English.

We can discuss "artistic or literary culture." We held our artists and storytellers in high esteem. Our arts are even now held in highest regard by noted artists of the world. Our literary works, while generally not written down, are only now being "discovered" as epics, examples of great beauty in

18

matry. We lived by our poets and storytellers, and many of them became our priests and leaders. The oratory of our leaders was superb, ringing with truth, eloquence and pride, and surely this is a high form of art. We revered our artists and historians, our literary men and women so much that when these arts were destroyed among the Maya and Inca people, the whole populace wept.

The architecture of the South American and Central American Tribes is only now being carefully examined for its extraordinary engineering, beauty and design. Our pottery, basket weaving, textile weaving, and metal-working has lent distinction and beauty to the arts of the whole world.

What was the "artistic or literary culture" of the strangers? They had no respect for their artists and authors. Indeed they brought with them no artistic articles, while we would have taken these with us as a first necessity. Their artists, even today, are underpaid and many excellent artists starve to death. With us, the artist and man of the oral literature and history was given full flow to his ideas, intelligence and creativity. Among the strangers, these people were tongue-lashed and even burned at the stake if they dared to express any thoughts opposed to the generally accepted dogmas.

"Marked by a tendency toward brutality, violence, or lawlessness," is another way the word *Barbarian* is described. These words mean different things to different people and races. To the men of the western so-called civilized countries like those Europeans who invaded our land, it means "typical of animals as distinct from man, based on crude animal instincts, grossly ruthless, devoid of mercy or compassion, cruel and cold-blooded, without human moderation, cruel (or even) stupid." The Indian resents this slur on the animal kingdom. I never knew an animal who abandoned her young, yet the Europeans have done it for centuries, even building special huge structures called "orphanages" to take care of the millions of children throughout the world who are deprived of their homes, beaten by grown men and women, or abandoned in a garbage can. What is "human moderation?" I don't see any signs of human moderation in the scalping activities of the Europeans, introduced by the Dutch. Our people took over this outrageous practice from the Anglos, and indeed in many respects some of our worst habits (such as drinking alcohol) were taken from the Europeans. Today, if the elders are not listened to, we Indians may become more like the Anglos every day, with all their worst habits and lack of "human moderation."

Historians point to the practice of human sacrifice among some tribes of the South American continent. They do not understand, that this was a religious practice, with meaning entirely different from that of the European culture. They might study about this, if they wish to be considered people of "learning." Some tribes of the eastern seaboard practiced forms of sacrifice of captives, after war became common among us following the European influences and intrusions. There is a unique and vastly misunderstood cultural meaning in this practice, which the Europeans would do well to study also. Certainly it was more "humane" than the currently accepted practice of bombing whole cities of innocent people, or spraying them with death-dealing chemicals, or machine-gunning mothers with babies in their arms, such as is being done today and has been done in the past by the "civilized" nations of the world.

Considering the last portion of the definition of *Barbarian*, which refers to "lawnessness," the history is filled with examples of the lawless practices of the white man in his relations with the Indian and with his relations with his own kind. The white man doesn't even respect his own courts, as witness the statement of President Andrew Jackson when informed of the decision of Supreme Court Justice John Marshall when he made a decision favoring the Cherokee Nation. Jackson said, "Marshall has made the decision; let him carry it out," and he proceeded to violate the decision of his own court. The illegal taking of Indian land; the illegal killing of Indian people; the illegal removal of Indian people from their homeland; and the illegal breaking of the white man's treaties with the Native Americans, even while the white man forced the Indian to sign the particular treaty, needs no footnotes, citations, or references in order to be substantiated.

The foreigners took our land, ignoring the fact that when we "gave" them a part of the earth, it was for use and not for sale. The word "inhumane" properly describes those early foreigners who came to our land, benefitted by our hospitality, and repaid our kindness with brutal disregard of our rights. The example is recalled, of Jamestown where we gave the Europeans a place to live on our land, depriving ourselves of the marvellous cornfields which had been in that earth. They repaid us when we were starving because our food stores had been destroyed, by giving us four hundred bushels of our own corn for that whole country.

The kinds and varieties of diseases brought to us by these foreigners destroyed whole tribes and villages. We thought these people must be rotting with corruption and degradation to have experienced such diseases, to such an extent that through the ages they became immune to them. But to us, with our clean bodies, our healthy and natural way of life, these diseases brought death and destruction.

Have we Indians received something from the Europeans, to make up for all these corrupt influences, lawless practices, and inhumane treatment? Yes. But I would not give one copper cent for the art of writing (which we would have developed anyhow, in our own way), the science of communications (when our communications among ourselves was much better than it is today, and more to be depended upon), or the flying machines, the riding machines, and the picture machines, for the magnificent continent they took from us brutally, lawlessly, violently, and inhumanely.

And so, in sum, we called these people *Barbarians*. Historically, they are Barbarians still.

Part III

Cultures in Conflict

THE WESTERN HEMISPHERE was wrested from the natives by means of military force, by fraud, and by genocide. It is not enough, however, to relate the facts of the ultimate disaster that overtook the natives. Without understanding how this came about, and unravelling the causes of the conflict in which this hemisphere and this nation became embroiled, we abrogate our responsibility to history, and deny our children their heritage.

The mode and means by which people make their living determines their social relationships, type of government, the nature of their culture, and even their religion. That is not to say that all peoples who depend upon the yield of natural resources, having a less sophisticated technology, will have the same government, society or religion. That is a generalization to be avoided. But the principal features of that culture will be very similar in such societies.

A people who depend for their subsistence upon the available game, fish, berries and fruits of their environment have a society distinguished by a minimum of government controls. Their social relationships are generally based upon the sort of economy they have developed, a subsistence economy. Thus, to take one example, there were some tribes in the region of California which made their living by hunting, fishing, and harvesting. One such society was comprised of eleven bands, each band with its own headman. The headmen of these bands then selected their leader, who came to be known by the Europeans, improperly, as a "chief." But he had little or no authority; he had only the rights of leadership by example, and by the advice he was considered capable of giving. Appearing before the Indian Claims Commission in 1965 was one such leader of his eleven bands. Asked by Commissioner Arthur Watkins how the Pitt River tribesmen elect their leaders, Mr. Ike Leaf replied: "If he knows where the fish swim, where the deer feed, where the rabbits run, he is a good leader, and if he knows how to show the way, he is a good leader and our headman by consent of all."

Such a people store their food for a future, when it may be scarce. They have no surplus of products, hence they do not sell. They do not consider their land as "property," hence they do not have a profit motive as to their land. Without their land they cannot live; and their land is revered, respected, cared for with love, and is a part of their religion. Their technology is geared to their way of life and to their arts. This type of society was multiplied many times over in North America before the coming of the Europeans. Some have considered life under such conditions as a sort of utopia, because the people respected life, one another, and their children, with the same love and care as they respected their Mother Earth.

Society is not a flat surface of matter, similar in all ways at all times. Change must be considered as a dynamic factor, and societies change and have changed, and continue to change, sometimes gradually over a span of thousands of years, sometimes quickly or even cataclysmically when there is an addition of certain new elements and conditions. But, at any point in time, the seeds of change already exist in each society. In a society such as we have just described, the seeds of change existed in the technological development of their husbandry, such as their manufacture of flint points, their industry of basket weaving, their labor of pottery-making. Once having satisfied their own needs, and set aside a store for the winter or against poor conditions of any kind, the Indians of that society began to have and produce more than they needed. Thus began the process of barter, in which one article of value is exchanged for another article of value, such value being measured by the needs or desires of the particular individuals engaged in the transaction.

When excess of available foods and articles of husbandry come to a certain high point, then begins the process of trade, in which an individual will exchange an article of pre-determined value for a quantity of other articles. After this, the appearance of forms of money is seen, in which one particular and recognizable article (such as dentalium or wampum) take on the property of a symbol for exchange. The people know that one string of wampum is worth (as a hypothesis) fifteen deerskins. The natives of that society are well on the road to change in their cultures, their type of government, and their social relationships. This perhaps labored explanation is necessary in order to explain what happened when the Indian people, with their various societies and their various economic systems, were confronted by a vastly different economy, a completely foreign concept of government, and an entirely different set of values. It needs to be stated once more, that the type of economy described above does not truly portray the economy existing among all the tribes of pre-European America. There were great variations in extent and complexity of technological development, great diversity in economic bases, and great differences in societal structure. As only one example, in the northwest of the present United States, a system of money as a form of exchange was already beginning to be seen. And the productivity of the tribal people had reached such an extent that the distribution of goods became a necessity. They developed a unique system of distribution of goods, and part of this system is to be seen in the traditional potlatch, in which goods were given away in a form of distribution which some scholars consider to have been a "game," or an excess of boastful show of wealth. They are wrong.

There is, however, one general thesis that can be accepted: wherever they lived, and whatever their economy, the Indian tribes of North America depended upon the land and its resources for their livelihood. There is scarcely a single native tongue in which there is not the phrase expressed one way or another, where the land is called "Mother Earth." Love and respect for the land was universal.

The Europeans who came either to settle or exploit the land and its people had a heritage of totally different economic conditions, an entirely different set of human and land values, an altogether different concept of government. The Europeans used money as an article of exchange, developed to such an extent that money itself had become a commodity to be kept, hoarded, and saved. Land was property, a thing to be owned. Language reflects the human condition and man's thought almost as much as his relations to his fellow man do. In European languages, one hears the inevitable phrase: One must earn one's living. That is the concept of profit and ownership at work. Because, if one is orphaned, elderly, or sick, then the conclusion must be that if you can't earn your living, you can't properly live. Let it be understood that English is a European language. It is not native to America.

European economy was based on exploitation of the land, accumulation of the means of production by a few, control over the economy by a ruling class, and the existence of money developed to such an extent that its symbol as *worth* and as *property* had become an entity unto itself and was accumulated for its own sake, also by the few. A system of feudalism existed, in which the major part of society labored for the ruling class, in exchange for which they received the bare minimum of life's necessities. The feudal serf was tied to the land and to its proprietor. He was a slave without visible shackles. The social relationships evolving from this type of economic condition bred a system of physical control over the serf by his master. The master or lord told him when and whether he could travel; when and whether he could remove to another lord's domain; whom he could marry and when. But within that European society there were already the seeds of change to another form of social relationships. Merchants and commerce began to emerge, with a totally different set of values. Commerce needed labor, lots of labor, and "free labor" was the clarion call of the day in the years when the Europeans began to settle in the land of the natives. Free labor made it possible for the merchant to draw from an army of laborers those he deemed best for the work, capable of working the hardest for the least in wages. Free labor became, in the end, the freedom to starve.

European economy was changing indeed, and the dynamics of that change wrought havoc within the ruling society and in the ranks of the workers and peasants who managed barely to survive under that rule. Debtors' prisons were filled to capacity. Disease because of extreme poverty and filth was rampant. Epidemics brought periodic holocausts of population decline. Political differences were intolerable to the monarchs and lords, and those who espoused the cause of the poor and destitute

25

were tortured, hanged, or burned at the stake for any reason not compatible with the philosophy of the ruling group.

The merchants, in that era, were the progressives of European society. They fought to free the economy from the iron grasp of the manor lords, the monarchists, and the church which ruled the rulers. They fought to free the serfs so that labor might be readily available. And they fought for a new system of government which would break the shackles of overlordship. Technological development was geared to such an economy. Looms for weaving, and factories where many workers labored, became a technological advance, so that more goods might be produced, more profits made, and so that the commercial interests might best be served.

With this baggage did the Pilgrims come to America: It consisted of an inherent philosophy of acquisition of goods and profits, an economic system of production for profit, and a government that ruled both in the physical as well as the spiritual realm. They had been forced to flee from intolerance in the mother country; but they practiced intolerance in the land of the natives. Many of them were escapees from debtors' prisons, but in Native America they became land grabbers, and despoilers of the native corn fields. Some were criminals sent to the "New World" in exile. In the land of the free native, they became exploiters and murderers without law and without respect for any human being other than their own brothers under the skin, criminals all. It would be wrong and unjust to assign such roles to all who came here. There were the people of courage, those of humane instincts, and those who tried to understand the native of this beautiful new land. They were among the few, and even they could not understand the way in which the native lived and believed about his land. One general philosophy pervaded all if not most of the immigrants: they believed in the theory that they had come to "vacant land," a land free from ownership, and that it was theirs for the taking.

The early explorations which sent Columbus and his cohorts on their way to find new worlds were not in the interests of pure science. They were an effort to find new markets for the powerful classes in Europe; they were an attempt to find new products to sell in Europe, for the acquisition of more profits, the adding of more property whether in goods or land.

The English came to take up native land, establish their towns and their government, and to produce sufficient for trade with the mother country. The Dutch came to establish the lu crative fur trade, and remained to "purchase" by fraud and deceit the Island of Manhattan and the town of Brooklyn. The French arrived and established colonies, intermarrying with native women, carrying on trade, engaging in the fur business and founding outposts of French dominion in Canada and the United States. The Spanish came to establish outposts of Imperial Spain in the new world, for purposes of profit, and domination on a world scale. The English and Spanish representatives of their monarchies, as a profitable side-line, developed the slave trade business, exporting the native peoples as beasts, and without hesitation separating families from one another with a cruelty comparable only to the launching of the atom bomb.

Thus, for some hundreds of years before and immediately following the arrival of the first Europeans on American soil, was Europe torn in many pieces with the turmoil of social and economic change, and the struggle for power among the monarchies, the merchant classes, the workingmen, the peasants, and the clergy.

It was inevitable that a clash of volcanic magnitude should take place in North and South America, between those with European standards of government and human values, and those natives with a totally different way of life and an entirely different economy.

Unfamiliar as they were with the European economic systems and European ideas of government, the natives were at first generally friendly. There was no way they could know that the use of their land, which they lent to the strangers as a matter of human decency, would be considered a "sale" and thereafter "belong to" the strangers. They did not have the philosophy expressed in the adage: "Beware of giving privileges, lest they be taken as rights."

Still another development took place, however, with the arrival of the Europeans with their greed for trade and furs. Immediately, the native became himself a prized commodity. It was the native who knew the land and the game. It was he who could lead the newcomers over the land and the streams. It was he who was the expert hunter, and it was the native, finally, who sold his hunting skills to the traders. With this new economic element, a cataclysmic change took place in the native society. Little recognized, stealing upon the Indian by night as it were, and in the dark of historic change, the change did come. It was dynamic, far-flung, overbearing in its influence upon all native life.

It was the competition for trade and new markets that made wars in the European countries. As trade begat war among the Europeans, so did the competition to supply that trade among the Indians beget wars, and intense rivalry existed among the tribes for the supply of the fur trade. They learned to sell a product. They learned that the fruits of those sales were good and great. They learned about iron tools, muskets and gunpowder. One thing they could not learn, for tradition and man's spiritual instincts die hard. That was the concept of their land as being capable of being sold. The Indian could not conceive that the earth could be sold. However, this knowledge also came to them with speed and accuracy, as the European laid his hands upon Indian land, claiming it and fighting for it against the defenders of that land.

With the breaking up of the Indian economy and the philosophy of human values that had become a part of that economy, it was also inevitable that other characteristics of European greed and infamy should make themselves felt. So it was that among the natives, traitors appeared, those who "sold" the land without the right to do so, those who came as pretenders to the role of "chieftainship," bestowed upon them by the foreigners. And Indian society underwent still more change and degradation as nation fought against nation for very survival. When the Europeans spread their propertied controls further into Indian territory, the tribes were pushed and shoved beyond their aboriginal borders. But the land was already well known and recognized as being in the domain of certain tribes, with designated tracts set aside for general and tribal use. Thus, various tribes were pushed onto the lands of tribes already inhabiting that land for thousands of years. The upheaval grew into a vast turmoil of tribe against tribe, people against people, and region against region.

Despite these monstrous conditions, the native people fought through the centuries for protection of their rights, and in defense of their land. This should be called the "Four Hundred Years' War," the longest war ever fought, as the natives, once irrevocably made aware of their situation and their imminent extinction as a race, rose up in defense of their land, their homes, their religion, and their people.

28

It did not take long for the native to decide that the immigrants would be his destruction, and to know with certainty that the gates of entry should have been closed to them so that the people might survive. War for the defense of their land took shape, and lasted for years. The Apaches fought a guerrilla war for two hundred years against immigrant encroachment. The Indian people of Ecuador and Peru drove out the Spaniards in the 16th century. The Natchez fought the French in 1727 and the Fox fought them in the Great Lakes country at approximately the same time. The Pawnees fought the Spanish to defend their land east of the Rockies in 1720. The Quechans of southern California and Arizona drove out the Spanish colonists in 1781. The Pueblos in 1680 rose in all the majesty of their anger over Spanish feudal serfdom and defeated them ignominiously. Only upon the request of some of the Pueblos were they able to return some years later. The Creeks utterly destroyed the Spanish missionary outposts of the Spanish empire in 1704, in the eastern part of the country. Metacom, (King Phillip) waged war against the intruders in 1675, displaying a statesmanship and martial genius that became the wonder of the European world. Books have been written and are still to be written describing the heroic struggle of the Native Americans against foreign oppression and the taking of their land.

The war of the Native was to last four hundred years, but slowly the American "frontier" overtook by conquest and fraud the native world, despite the 370 treaties made between the 18th to the 19th centuries. This was a conflict of native people against foreign intrusion. But it was more than that, it was a conflict of cultures, one vastly different than the other.

America now lives in a culture dominated by the European system of economy, the European system of government only slightly altered to conform to the example set by the great Iroquois confederacy. Is this dominant culture more desirable than that of the native? Looking backward, we can hypothesize that if the native had been treated differently, justly, there might now exist a culture constituting an amalgam of the best of two worlds. It was not to be.

Part IV

The Treaty Era
in
Indian History

THERE ARE STILL those who refuse to accept the fact that the natives of this hemisphere had established nations, recognized as such by international law, by European governments seeking to establish outposts of power in the new world, by the colonists prior to the establishment of the United States, and by the United States government before and following the adoption of the constitution.

There are those who claim: 1) That recognition of the Indians as nations, and the making of treaties with them, was merely a "face-saving" device utilized by the United States to gain the support of the native tribes at critical times in the history of the young United States; or 2) That the recognition of Indian peoples as nations and the making of treaties is "ancient history," no longer applicable in modern social and legal relations. Under this latter theory, Indian treaties have no force today, and this is the philosophy guiding the extermination policy, however well such a policy may be disguised.

An analysis of international law and relationships with

European powers prior to the establishment of the American government, is not within the scope of this article. What is being considered here is the relationship of the United States with the Indians following establishment of the federal government. Clearly the government continued to deal with the Indians as nations. In legislation enacted in 1789, the first year of the first Congress, four statutes dealing with Indian affairs bore practical recognition of the Indian nations: The Act of August 7, 1789, establishing the Department of War, assigned to that department matters "relative to Indian affairs." A second statute dealing with the Northwest Territory provided that ". . . the utmost good faith shall always be observed towards the Indians; their land and property shall never be taken from them without their consent; and in their property, rights, and liberty, they shall never be disturbed, unless in just and lawful wars authorized by Congress . . ." A third act of Congress was the Act of August 20, 1789, appropriating money to negotiate treating with the Indian tribes. On September 11, 1789, the Congress established salaries to be paid to the Superintendent of Indian Affairs, a position held by the governor of the western territory ex officio. This first Congress enacted legislation establishing territorial or state governments for thirty-five states admitted to the Union. These states contained a concentration of nearly all the Indians remaining as tribes at the time of the adoption of the Constitution. As Felix Cohen sums it up, (Handbook of Indian Law): "In these four statutes we find the essential administrative machinery for dealing with Indian affairs established: . . . the power to make war (and, presumably, peace); the power to govern territories; the power to make treaties; and the power to spend money." Thus was the *internal* machinery established on the part of the United States, *on the federal level*, and the Indian nations as a responsibility of the federal government, were recognized and are still so recognised today. Efforts of the states and local governments to break away, piece by piece, the authority and the rights of the Indian nations, has been and is today at the very center of the Indian resistance to extermination. The efforts to institute another "removal policy," continue on behalf of private interests seeking Indian water, Indian natural resources, and to deny Indian rights to self-determination, and Indian existence as viable economic tribal communities.

The native peoples, from whom a whole continent has been

taken, remain in areas containing the merest fraction of what was once their land. Even now, defense of that pitiful remainder requires the full energy and vigilance of the tribes. In the process of protecting these lands, the rights of the tribes as expressed in the three hundred and seventy-one treaties are being defended. It should be recognized, however, that the treaties themselves were instruments of expropriation, extermination, and dispossession.

It is impossible to read the texts of the treaties without experiencing a horror and dismay at what has been done to the original owners of this land. Kappler's "Indian Treaties" ought to be required reading for all those who study American history. Here one can trace the expropriation of tribe after tribe from their ancestral homes. A general review of what happened through the treaties may be in order.

Through treaties with the Indian nations, the United States extorted privileges and expropriated land. The deed was done by these means: Through demanding and obtaining, often at gun point, "free passage over Indian lands." Such free passage became rights to land taken unilaterally by the federal government. Cessions of Indian land were made through the treaties, to the United States, and in treaty after treaty, if one follows those made with any tribe, is to be found more and more land whittled away, expropriated from the Indian tribe, the land described by metes and bounds. Forts were established through treaties, the right to build such forts being written into the treaty, the land then becoming property of the United States. Around these forts were portions of land established as the "property of the United States," as, for example in the treaty with the Six Nations of October 22, 1784, in which it was stated that ". . . the Six Nations shall and do yield to the United States, all claims to the country west of the said boundary, . . . reserving six miles square around the Fort of Oswego to the United States."

On January 21, 1785, in a treaty with the Wyandot, Delaware, and Chippewa Nations, the United States reserved "six miles square . . . for the establishment of trading posts," six more miles square at the "portage of the Big Miami River, six miles square on Sandusky Lake, and two miles square on each side of the lower rapids of the Sandusky."

On September 17, 1778, however, in a treaty with the Delawares, the first treaty made by the United States with an In-

dian nation, the United States agreed that they ". . . do en
gage to guarantee to the aforesaid nation of Delawares, and
their heirs, all their territorial rights in the fullest and most
ample manner . . ."

A treaty with the Cherokee Nation on November 28, 1785,
established boundaries recognized by the United States as en-
compassing land belonging to that Nation. But on July 2, 1791,
these boundaries were changed in favor of more land ceded to
the United States, and again the United States declared in the
words of this second treaty, which was ratified by the Senate,
that "The United States solemnly guarantee to the Cherokee
Nation all their lands not hereby ceded." Through the years
to come, down through the infamous Removal Act of 1830 and
its subsequent forced eviction of the Cherokee people from their
ancestral homes, other treaties were made with this Indian Nation, and each new treaty extracted more and more land from
the native people.

Examples of the devious way in which this expropriation
was carried out, is expressed in the many treaties which amended previous treaties, because, as was explained in several
treaties made with the Cherokees, the conditions of the previous
treaty "were not carried out," thus making it possible to enforce another treaty, and in this subsequent treaty, more land
was expropriated through "cession" of the tribe to the United
States.

Expropriation of land was a major purpose behind the signing of treaties with the Indian nations. There were other reasons for the United States to make treaties with the owners of
the continent. The United States desperately needed either support or neutralization of the Indian tribes. Treaty-making was
a means to this end. We now consider the treaties in the history of the American Indian.

When contact was first made with the natives of North
America by the Europeans, they came as friends. At least, on
our part we considered them as friends, and we helped them.
Conficts arose, however, largely because of two vastly different
systems of government, two different systems of economy,
great differences in values and government. These differences
were only accentuated with time, and within one century after
the first entry into the North American continent, conflict became war.

Skirmishes occurred around localities wanted by the whites.

Wars occurred because there were Indian leaders who saw that they would lose their land if the conflicts were not resolved in favor of the original owners of the land.

What is significant, however, is that at a very early date there were Europeans who attempted to resolve the differences, in order to gain an economic and political foothold in America. These attempts took the form of trade agreements, treaties of peace and friendship, treaties to settle land ownership, and treaties made as a result of conquest by the Europeans.

A *Treaty* is defined in Webster's unabridged dictionary as "a contract in writing between two or more political authorities (as states or sovereigns), formally signed by representatives duly authorized and usually ratified by the lawmaking authority." For example, the United States Constitution stipulates that ". . . the President . . . shall have power, by and with the advice and consent of the Senate, to make treaties . . ."

Black's law dictionary states that a treaty, in international law, is "a compact made between two or more independent nations with a view to the public welfare." Or, as he further states, "An agreement, league, or contract between two or more nations or sovereigns, formally signed by commissioners properly authorized, and solemnly ratified by the several sovereigns or the supreme power of each state." A treaty of peace, it is stated by the same authority, is "an agreement or contract made by belligerent powers, in which they agree to lay down their arms, and by which they stipulate the conditions of peace and regulate the manner in which it is to be restored and supported." It is stated also, in the same section of Black that there is a difference between "Personal" treaties, and "Real" treaties, and the wording is quite clear: "As distinguished from *Personal* treaties, *Real* treaties relate solely to the subject matters of the convention (convention here means the instrument itself, the treaty) independently of the persons of the contracting parties, and continue to bind the state, although there may be changes in the constitution or in the persons of the rulers."

This discussion is necessary, because there has been from the beginning a lack of clarity as to just what a treaty with the Indian Nations is. There are some who say that this "was just a face-saving device." There are others who state that the treaties are "antique instruments," with no validity any longer. None of this is true. The treaties and agreements made with

34

the Indian Nations are valid, enforceable, and can only be invalidated by a formal Act of the congress of the United States.

Adding to the complexity of the treaty-making relationships between the United States government, there are these questions to consider:

Treaties made in the early stages of American governmental activities were amended and changed with time. Agreements which were made served to modify treaties. Treaties made with a group of tribes were later modified and amended, not necessarily with the entire group, but with certain individual tribes or parts of that original group. Treaties were made with representatives of the various tribes, but not "by authorized representatives" of the tribe, and thus questions may be raised as to the validity of that treaty or that modification of the treaty, or that agreement. In such a case, the United States government does not have a treaty, and charges can be made and proven in litigation, that the land was therefore taken without consent, and without payment which would extinguish title to the land. The same condition prevails if the Indian signers did not understand, or could not read. Evidence of fraudulent interpreters are common.

The whole question of the Indian treaty relationship with the United States is filled with complexities. One thing is perfectly clear. That is, that the treaties were made as between nations, both internationally recognized, and recognized by the federal government. Cases have been filed in litigation against the United States by tribes, then adjudicated in the courts, and then many years later, the tribes have come back into court with still another claim, stating that the first settlement was made in an "inadequate amount," that the Indian people who authorized that settlement were unaware of the fraud practiced by government agents, or any number of other situations.

Certainly both the United States and the Indian tribes will come face to face with the necessity to resolve the entire question, at some time in the future. Opinions differ widely as to just what such a settlement should be. However, no matter what the conditions of settlement may be, one thing comes clearly into focus as the tribes and reservations continue to battle in the courts, being placed in the unconscionable position of having to go from one court to another, to expend money and energy, and be bounced like a yo-yo from one court case to another: That is, that the Indian people were cheated, and

35

indeed were in fact, sovereign nations.

It is therefore of utmost importance that at least a minimal understanding be developed, of the unique relationship between the American Indian and the federal government, as well as just what the treaties involve and what they were.

The first treaty of which there is any record, is one that was made long before the establishment of the United States government. This was the Treaty of Tawagonshi, made in 1613 between the Dutch and the Iroquois people. Explaining this legal instrument is Dr. L. G. Van Loon, who wrote the article here reprinted from The Indian Historian.

Other treaties and agreements were made between the Indians and the French, the Indians and the Dutch, and the Indians in agreements with the British government. But those which are of great concern are the ones made between the United States and the Indian tribes. Such treaties began in 1778, with the Delawares. This treaty is particularly significant in the history of the Indian, because the Delawares were promised they could be constituted as a *state*, within the United States. If this doesn't prove that the government treated with us as *Nations*, then let the historian beware, because he is tampering with hard and provable facts.

The last treaty made with the Indian Nations was with the Nez Perces, in 1868. This instrument was an amendment to an earlier treaty made with the same nation in 1863.

Efforts of the federal government to claim the entire continent continued well into the end of the 19th Century. The Indians, however, stood in the path of empire. These complex political as well as economic situations had an effect upon the United States Congress, which soon began to quarrel as to who had the right to ratify or negotiate treaties with the Indian Nations. The Senate, which had the right, as stipulated in the Constitution, to "advise and consent" to treaties, insisted upon appropriations for carrying out treaties. But the House refused to grant funds for the purpose. The situation was resolved, finally, when, in the Indian Appropriation Act of 1871, making an appropriation for the Yankton Sioux, a clause was inserted in the Act, ending all treaty making.

But agreements continued to be made; amendments to treaties continued to be negotiated; and reservations continued to be set aside either by Executive presidential order, or by Executive congressional order. Nothing had really been solved.

The United States is firmly committed, by laws of its own, and by international law, to see to it that "treaty enforcement continues . . . and that there shall be no lessening of obligations already incurred." This statement was made by Felix Cohen, in *Handbook of Indian Law*, published by the federal government, and approved by the Department of Justice. In the same volume, Cohen observes, "That treaties with Indian tribes are of the same dignity as treaties with foreign nations is a view which has been repeatedly confirmed by the federal courts and never successfully challenged."

In this chapter, we shall give examples of certain treaties which are of historic significance, and we begin with the Tawagonshi treaty. Next, we quote the first treaty made with the Delawares in 1778; and finally the last treaty (an amendment) made with the Nez Perces in 1868.

There is certainly no intention of presenting a comprehensive treatment of the treaties, or the treaty-making relationship between the federal government the the American Indian. Only the outlines can be given here, and a guide to further study.

The Treaty of Tawagonshi

L. G. VAN LOON, M.D.

During the course of history, many treaties and conventions have been consummated between representatives of the Caucasian western European and the American Indian. The subject of the article is an early treaty made between western Europeans and representatives of the Iroquois Nation of Indians. This treaty, or convention, is perhaps the first recorded attempt on the part of the whites to secure by "fair" bargaining, a peaceful foothold in the new land. Because of the absence of any specific reference to it, the treaty has remained practically unknown.

Made by two Dutch traders with the Iroquois in 1613 at Tawagonshi (approximately in the vicinity of Albany), the treaty is also interesting because it was an agreement which the Indians faithfully tried to maintain for perhaps one hundred and sixty years, even though successive white regimes disregarded it.

Five Iroquois tribes occupied the banks of the Mohawk River in New York at the coming of the white man, in the following order from the east to west: the Mohawk or Canienga; Oneida or Onenniot; Onondaga or Anontage; Cayuga or Ko'yu'kwen', and Seneca or Sonontowane. Related to them ethnically and in known times subject to them politically, were the Eries, the Attiwandaronks of "Neutral Nation," the Conestogas, and the Hurons. A distant branch of the Iroquois stock called Tuscarora was driven from North Carolina and joined the principal "Five Nations" early in the 18th century to make up the famous "Six Nations" by which name they are known to the present day.

At the height of their power the Iroquois exerted a strong influence over adjacent tribes occupying portions of French Canada, New England, Pennsylvania, and Ohio as well as having obvious control in the state of New York. Various estimates of their numerical strength have been given, between the time of the first colonization by western Europeans up to and including the present. Greenhalgh reported on a journey made through their country in 1677, that the "Maques" (the early Low Dutch name for Mohawks) "pass in all for about 300 fighting men...

38

(the Oneidas) . . . are said to have about 200 fighting men . . . The Onondaga pass for about 350 fighting men . . . (the Cayugas) . . . pass for about 300 fighting men . . . and the Seneeques are counted to be in all about 1,100 fighting men."

This might give a somewhat arbitrary figure of 4,250 as a total population. In 1763, Sir William Johnson, His Majesty's superintendent for Indian Affairs in North America, living in the heart of the Mohawk country, reported on each Indian group living within his jurisdiction, and the total number of men for the Iroquois group at that time, including the Tuscarora, was given at 1,950. Thus, an idea as to the possible fluctuation in the number of fighting men in the course of one hundred years may be had.

The development of Iroquois power over surrounding nations of Indians which occurred in the first decades of the 18th century, was brought about by their strategic position between the forces of New France to the north and the ever apprehensive Dutch, and later the English in the province of New York and to the south, a position which they exploited as best they could by acting as suppliers to the fur traders on both sides, and acting as buffers during the times of actual or threatened invasion.

The political bond which drew all five tribes together was unique among the inhabitants of Indian American, and was certainly equal to any similar pact by so-called civilized nations elsewhere in the world. The "League of the Iroquois" was a remarkable achievement indeed, the details of which will not concern us in this article. Suffice it to say that, so far as tradition was concerned, it had its inception some time in the middle of the 15th century under the aegis of an honored chief of the Onondagas, later adopted by the Mohawks: Hiawatha. By it, the Iroquois tribes were welded into a fairly cohesive political unit which served them well until the final downfall of the Iroquoian Confederacy at the termination of the Revolutionary War. The scattered bands revived the League thereafter, and it has been maintained as a historical tradition since. It served its makers well, in its time; so much so, that the Iroquois were a Confederation that had to be reckoned with.

By the end of the 17th century, the power of the Confederacy had reached such proportions that Governor Dugan wrote, in a report of the Committee of Trade in 1687, "The five Indian Nations are the most warlike people in America, and are a bullwark between us and the French and all other Indians . . . "

Certainly the Iroquois had some knowledge of the earliest coming of the foreigners, since it was in 1535 that Cartier sailed up the St. Lawrence River. Hudson, too, penetrated very early in 1600 to the upper reaches of the river now bearing his name. In 1609, Hudson went up the river approximately to the area where Albany now lies, perhaps further. In the same year, Champlain came down from New France along the trail which followed the shore of the lake named after him, accompanied by a small war party of Indians. Instead of being laden with trade goods, Champlain was burdened with weapons, and when his party eventually met a small band of Iroquois, this Gallic warrior propped up his arquebuss and let off a thunderous charge which did some damage to the Iroquois. This single volley made implacable enemies of the tribe.

After Hudson's journey of exploration, considerable interest developed in Europe as to the possibilities of trade in that area of the new continent. In many cases the traders were individuals who had the equipment and the fortitude necessary to cross the Atlantic and engage in barter. In other cases, they were financed by some other individual, who provided the equipment but lacked the time or incentive to trade and explore in person. The spring of the year 1613 found two Dutch gentlemen, probably trading under these latter conditions, near the location of the present city of Albany at the Indian site of Tawagonshi, who negotiated a treaty with the Iroquois nation. The writer has translated from the original Dutch, an exact English language translation of this treaty.

This document, which appears to be a compact binding the Iroquois with a Dutch Company through its agents, was written upon two pieces of hide. It roughly measures seven and a half inches by thirteen inches, when the two pieces are placed to approximate each other, along what would be the midline. The two pieces may have been at one time a single piece, or may have been sewn together along this midline at some other time.

The "Treaty of Tawagonshi" was procured through an individual who was the agent on the Missisaqua Reservation in Canada many years ago. When, and under what circumstances it was originally acquired, is unknown at this time. Undoubtedly the importance of the document was not appreciated. Referring as it does to the past of the Iroquois, it brings to mind the attempt on the part of members of the Iroquois band at Ohswe-

kun to salvage some of their tribal records from their head-
quarters before the infamous raid by Canadian officials, aided
by a cordon of Mounties in 1924, when they carried off much
that was important and dear to the Iroquois. In any case, the
"Treaty of Tawagonshi" does much to explain the sequence of
events which led to the kind of political action the Iroquois
took at the outbreak of the Revolutionary War, when they supported the British cause. If it be genuine, or if it is not, will
make little difference so far as the contents are concerned. The
matter of the contents, which have a definite historic validity,
is what this article is all about.

Jacob Eelckens and Hendrick Christianssen were the two
Dutch traders who signed as agents for the company which
they no doubt represented. They were known to have been in
the business of trading. Very little personally as to appearance
and character is known of either man, although Eelckens is
referred to several times in the Rensselaer-Bowier records.
Christiaenssen is spoken of in De Laet's Journal. They were
representative of what may have been a group plying up and
down the coast of Lower New England, Long Island Sound,
the Hudson River, and the South (Delaware) River in their
tiny vessels, seeking out the Indian and his inevitable bundle
of furs with which business could be done. Who sent, or commissioned them? The premise that they were either sent or
commissioned is implied in the wording of the treaty, as to
the purpose of granting such authority as they possessed under
the document.

De Roever states in his article "Kiliaen van Rensselaer
and his Colony Rensselaerswyck" that the West Indian Company had its charter granted "after long years of preparation
. . . June 3, 1621," a date which is later than the date of this
Treaty by eight years. Hartgers related that Hudson sent his
information on the great river he had explored to his employers
in 1609, and that they in turn sent out a trading ship in 1610.
Later, in 1614, they received permission from the natives at
about the location of the present city of Albany, to erect a
fort and trading post. The earliest dates described by Hartgers
may refer to the activities of the New Netherland Company
formed by merchants of Amsterdam and Hoorn, which received
a three-year monopoly on trade in 1614. At the expiration of
the monopoly of the New Netherland Company in 1618, a new
charter was refused. Only private venture was conceived until

41

1621, when the West Indian Company received its charter.

It is quite probable that this Treaty may have been executed originally for the benefit of the New Netherland Company or for one or more of its members. Apparently, use was made of any one of this agreements provisions, and that is implied in the statement giving "permission" to erect a fort and trading post at Castle Island. The short term of this charter would militate against the purchase of any land. The chronology here is within reason. If the Amsterdam and Hoorn merchants were inclined to set up in the trading business in what is now New York State after the glowing report the East Indian Company had received from Hudson, and especially after the return of the successful trading voyage in 1610, it would have been possible to strengthen their American position by consummating some core of agreement.

Hendrick Christiaenssen and Jacob Eelckens were the officers in charge of the first trading post in 1614 as stated in Hartgers account, published in 1642. The ultimate career of these two worthies is lost. Eelckens was later apparently a skipper for one "Hontum" and as late as 1634 was referred to by van Rensselaer as "one of the merchants in Amsterdam."

Inquiries made to available Iroquoian historians, and to the offices of both the Canadian and American agencies concerned with Indian Affairs, have met with either ignorance or silence, on the subject of the 1613 treaty. In contemporary historical works, reference is only made to an early treaty having been concluded with the Indians. There is only the physical evidence of the treaty itself, its language. However, there are many references to an "early treaty" made by the Iroquois chiefs prior to the Revolutionary War in statements principally made by the Indians themselves. Such references nearly always mention the "Covenant of the silver chain," the "Covenant of the chain," the "chain which binds our people together," or the "chain which we will forever keep bright." Is this language merely metaphorical? Or does it indeed refer, time and again, to the last paragraph of the "Treaty of Tawagonshi," in which it is stated, ". . . and as evidence of the honor and goodwill we exchange a silver chain for a fathom of beadwork"?

In the mid-1650's, members of the Iroquoian delegation were meeting with the magistrates of the Dutch community of Fort Orange (Albany) and referring to the treaty that was "already old" between the two peoples, and to the "chain" which bound the two peoples together.

This allusion is also to be found in the Sir William Johnson manuscripts and used by numbers of Iroquoian orators, nearly to the end of Johnson's term of office at the time of his death. The actions of the Indians, as a political unit, through the years up to the outbreak of the Revolutionary War, seem to imply that they felt the changeover from Dutch rule to British only served to transfer their allegiance from the Dutch to the British in a legal and comprehensible way. With the later deterioration of relations between the colonies and England, at the time when the colonists chose to fight for freedom, the Indians found themselves in the middle of the controversy. For the most part, the tribes had gotten along quite well with the colonists, so far as affairs on the Upper Hudson and the reaches of the Mohawk river were concerned. They owed an old allegiance to the English, tracing back through the days when the "Skaghneghtadaronni" (Iroquois name for the Dutch) were the authorities with whom they had sat down and agreed that they were to be bound together by a "silver chain" for all time.

There came a time when the Indians felt that they had sided with the wrong party. At the treaty of Fort Stanwix, the Iroquois discovered that they now owned little or nothing of what were once their vast tribal holdings in the state of New York. There was little for them to do, other than to find a future home in a land still under the authority of England-Canada. But this deal was one in which the Indians soon found that generosity was not a characteristic of the whites. The paltry acreage of reservations they received in Canada was scarcely a fair exchange for their sacrifices in lands in New York, while adhering to their own ideas of integrity and honor.

Nearly three hundred and sixty-five years have passed since Henry Hudson made known to Europeans the wondrous advantages of the River and its adjacent lands. It is curious that even at this date the Treaty of Tawagonshi should still be unnoticed and unknown. Perhaps this bit of hide upon which is written the conditions of an ancient agreement in the Dutch tongue, will open up avenues of historical inquiry, to answer some of the questions raised in this article. Certainly the period encompassed in the years immediately after the Tawagonshi event were famed for the freedom from strife between Indian and white man. Many Indians were welcome in the kitchens of the colonists, took bread there, and considered the colonists as friends. A small amount of intermarriage took place also. And many Indians learned to speak Low Dutch.

This writer need only say, finally, to those descendants of the Iroquoians who made the gracious gesture of welcome at Tawagonshi, that the story of their forefathers is known and respected, especially by the descendants of those friendly Dutch who received the Tawagonshi gesture of peace and friendship.

The Treaty

Here at Tawagonshi met with us the undersigned Jacob Eelckens and Hendrick Christiaenssen, authorized by letter and obligated to examine into the trade with the aboriginal owners or directors of the country hereabouts and to conclude, as far as it may be compatible with the following chiefs of the Long House, Gerhatjannie, Caghneghsattakegh, Otskwiragerongh, and Teyoghswegengh, as well as other lesser chiefs of the same who declare that they are all in agreement thereupon, and we the participants promise: 1, That trade between their people and ours shall be permitted as long as we the participants are bilaterally agreed, and further; 2, That we the participants shall have the privilege of bringing our goods out of trade channels as long as no purchase agreement concerning them has been made: and further; 3, Parcels of land may be purchased that we the aboriginal participants consider as our property so long as it is discussed by the individuals and a bilaterally agreeable purchase agreement concerning them has been made, and further; 4, That we the participants shall be obliged to help each other to necessities in case of shortage of food that is insufficient, and further; 5, In case of a difference of opinion concerning real or imaginary injustices we the participants promise that this will stand as an Auspicia Melioris Aevi and that any difference from whatever nature or origin must be brought before a meeting of Commissaries in order to examine the whole. This foregoing we the participants promise in love and friendship to continue and to maintain for as long as grass is green and as evidence of the honor and goodwill we exchange a silver chain for a fathom of beadwork; and knowledge of the truth of this here undersigned by the participants on this 21st April 1613.

The Treaty With the Delawares

This first treaty made by the young United States government, was signed September 17, 1778, and is worded as follows:

That all offenses or acts of hostilities by one or either of the contracting parties against the other be mutually forgiven, and buried in the depth of oblivion. And that a perpetual peace and friendship shall from henceforth take place, and subsist between the contracting parties aforesaid, through all succeding generations: and if either of the parties are engaged in a just and necessary war with any other nation or nations, that then each shall assist the other in due proportion to their abilities, till their enemies are brought to reasonable terms of accomodation; and that if either of them shall discover any hostile designs forming against the other, they shall give the earliest notice thereof, that measures may be taken to prevent their ill effect.

Whereas the United States are engaged in a just and necessary war in defence and support of life, liberty and independence, against the King of England and his adherents, and as said King is yet possessed of several posts and forts on the lakes and other places, the reduction of which is of great importance to the peace and security of the contracting parties, and as the most practicable way for the troops of the U.S. to some of the posts and forsts is by passing through the country of the Delaware nation, the aforesaid deputies, on behalf of themselves and their nation, do hereby stipulate and agree to give a free passage through their country to the troops aforesaid, and the same to conduct by the nearest and best ways to the posts, forts or towns of the enemies of the U.S., affording to said troops such supplies of corn, meat, horses, or whatever may be in their power for the accommodation of such troops, on the commanding officer's paying or engaging to pay, the full value of whatever they can supply them with.

And the said deputies, on behalf of their nation, engage to join the troops of the United States aforesaid, with such number of their best and most expert warriors as they can spare, consistent with their own safety, and act in concert with them; and for the better security of the old men, women and children of the aforesaid nation, whilst their warriors are engaged against the common enemy, it is agreed on the part of the United States, that a fort of sufficient strength and capacity be built at the expense of the said States, with such assistance as it may be in the power of the said Delaware Nation to give, in the most convenient place, and advantageous situation, as shall be agreed upon by the commanding officer of the troops aforesaid, with the advice and concurrence of the deputies of the aforesaid Delaware Nation, which fort shall be garrisoned by such a number of the troops of the United States as the commanding officer can spare for the present, and hereafter by such numbers, as the wise men of the United States in council, shall think most conducive to the common good.

Neither party shall proceed to the infliction of punishments on the citizens of the other, otherwise than by securing the offender or offenders by imprisonment, or any other competent means, till a fair and impartial trial can be had by judges or juries of both parties, as near as can be to the laws, customs and usages of the contracting parties and natural justice. The mode of such trials to be hereafter fixed by the wise men of the United States in Congress assembled, with the assistance of such deputies of the Delaware Nation, as may be appointed to act in concert with them in adjusting this matter to their mutual liking.

(Both parties agreed to deliver up enemies of either or both, to the United States, or to the states or state to which "such enemies, criminals, servants or slaves respectively belong.")

(A well regulated trade was engaged upon by the United States with the Delawares, to provide them with articles such as clothing, utensils and implements of war, from time to time.)

Whereas the enemies of the United States have endeavored, by every article in their power, to possess the Indians in general with an opinion, that it is the design of the States aforesaid, to extirpate the Indians and take possession of their country; to obviate such false suggestion, the United States do engage to guarantee to the aforesaid Nation of Delawares and their heirs, all their territorial rights in the fullest and most ample manner, as it hath been bounded by former treaties, as long as they the said Delaware Nation shall abide by, and hold fast the claim of friendship now entered into.

It is further agreed on between the contracting parties, that should it for the future be found conducive for the mutual interest of both parties to invite any other tribes who have been friends to the interest of the United States to join the present confederation, and to form a state whereof the Delaware Nation shall be the head, and have a representative in Congress: Provided, nothing contained in this article to be considered as conclusive until it meets with the approbation of Congress. And it is also the intent and meaning of this article, that no protection or countenance shall be afforded to any who are at present our enemies, by which they might escape the punishment they deserve.

This treaty was signed at Fort Pitt, September 17, 1778, by Andrew Lewis, Thomas Lewis, White Eyes, The Pipe, and John Kill Buck, in the presence of eleven military officers of the United States Army.

The Treaty With the Nez Perces

Whereas certain amendments are desired by the Nez Perce Tribe of Indians to their treaty concluded at the council ground in the valley of the Lapwai, in the Territory of Washington, in the ninth day of June, 1863; and whereas the United States are willing to assent to the amendments, it is therefore agreed by and between Nathanial G. Taylor, commissioner, on the part of the United States, and Lawyer, Timothy and Jason, chiefs of said tribe, that:

All lands embraced within the limits of the tract set apart for the exclusive use and benefit of said Indians by the 2nd article of said treaty of June 9, 1863, which are susceptible of cultivation and suitable for Indian farms, which are not now occupied by the United States for military purposes or which are not required for agency or other buildings and purposes provided for in said treaty, and as soon as the allotments shall be plowed and fenced, and as soon as schools shall be established as provided by existing treaty stipulations, such Indians now residing outside the reservation as may be decided upon by the agent of the tribe and the Indians themselves, shall be removed to and located upon allotments within the reservation.

Provided, however, that in case there should not be a sufficient quantity of suitable land within the boundaries of the reservation to provide allotments for those now there and those residing outside the boundaries of the same, then those residing outside, or as many thereof as allotments cannot be provided for, may remain upon the lands now occupied and improved by them, provided that the land so occupied does not exceed 20 acres for each and every male person who shall have attained the age of 21 years or is the head of a family, and the tenure of those remaining upon lands outside the reservation shall be the same as is provided in said third article of said treaty, for those receiving allotments within the reservation.

It is further agreed between the parties hereto that the stipulations contained in the 8th article of the treaty, relative to timber, are hereby annulled as far as the same provides that the United States shall be permitted to use thereof in the maintaining of forts or garrisons, and that the said Indians shall have the aid of the military authorities to protect the timber upon their reservation, and that none of the same shall be cut or removed without the consent of the head-chief of the tribe, together with the consent of the agent and superintendent of Indian affairs, first being given in writing, which written consent shall state the part of the reservation upon which the timber is to be cut and also the quantity, and the price to be paid therefor.

It is further stipulated that the amount due said tribe for school purposes and for the support of teachers that has not been expended for that purpose since the year 1864, but has been used for other purposes, shall be ascertained and the same shall be reimbursed to said tribe by appropriation by Congress, and shall be held in trust by the U.S., the interest on the same to be paid to said tribe annually for the support of teachers.

(This document was signed by "chiefs representing" the Nez Perce tribe on August 31, 1868, in Washington, D.C.)

Signatories were: N. G. Taylor, commissioner of Indian Affairs, Lawyer, head chief, Nez Perces; Timothy, chief; and Jason, chief.

The treaty amendment was ratified February 16, 1869.

(Kappler's Treaties, is the source for this data. All treaties and agreements are published in this 6-volume set generally titled: "Laws and Treaties.")

Treaties of the Sioux

Examples have been given of the first treaty made between the Indians and the United States, and the last treaty made, before the official treaty period ended in 1871. An examination of the Delawares, those of the first treaty, will show that treaty-making with them did not end in 1778 with that first nation-to-nation document. Numbers of other treaties were made with them.

This situation is true of all the tribes. With each new treaty, more land was taken, more restrictions were imposed upon the natives, and more of their sovereign rights as nations were taken away. The later treaties are shocking in their complete disregard for the rights of human beings. The natives became strangers in their own land. Fraud was practived in the signing of treaties. The signers were generally not authorized by the tribes to do so. Finally, the tribes were made to sign treaties which could be unilaterally voided or changed beyond recognition by the United States Senate. With all these conditions, however, certain rights still exist in the treaties, and their observance is a matter of national and international law.

A prime example of this outrageous treatment of the natives exists in the treaties made with the Sioux people. At least thirty-two treaties were made with the Sioux. In some cases these were made with certain bands of the tribe. In other cases they were lumped together with other tribes. And, with each new treaty, more and more land was whittled away, more and more rights were destroyed, more and more restrictions were imposed. Certainly this kind of injustice cannot help but leave its mark upon a people who were shuttled from one place to another, removed from their vast homeland, left to starve and freeze without food, without clothing, and without a way of life.

The Sioux rebelled. Certainly they rebelled. Indeed the patience of these people is a model of international self-respect. But finally, the slender thread of human endurance broke, and they made war against those who had deprived them of culture, economy, and life itself.

Still there are remnants of their rights as nations left in the treaties. These rights at least, must be recognized, and these treaties, so long violated, must now be inforced and respected.

It would serve the reader well, in creating a knowledge based upon historic truth, as well as a means of understanding the current movement of the Sioux people, to examine carefully the following "Saga of the Sioux" in the process of treaty-making with the United States government. It is but one example of the way in which the federal government dealt with the native tribes of this their native land.

July 19, 1815, Treaty of peace and friendship with the Teton at Portage des Sioux. Signed by Eskatapia, the Player; Tantanga, the True Buffalo; Weechachamanza, the Man of Iron; Ikmouacoulai, the Shooting Tiger; Uakahincoukai, the Wind that Passes; Mazamanie, the Walker in Iron; Wanakagmamee, the Stamper; Washeejonjrtga, the Left Handed Frenchman; and Monetowanari, the Bear's Soul.

July 19, 1815, Treaty of peace and friendship with the Sioux of the Lakes at Portage des Sioux. Signed by William Clark, Ninian Edwards, Auguste Chouteau, Tatangamania, Walking Buffalo; Haisanwee, the Horn; Aampahaa, the Speaker; Narcesagata, the Hard Stone, Haibohaa, the Branching Horn.

July 19, 1815, Treaty of peace and friendship with the Sioux of St. Peter's River at Portage des Sioux. Signed by Enigmanee, that Flies as he Walks; Wasoukapaha, Falling Hail; Champisaba, Black War Club; Manpinsaba, Black Cloud; Tatarnaza, Iron Wind; Nankanandee, who Puts His Foot in it.

July 19, 1815, Treaty of peace and friendship with the Yankton Sioux at Portage des Sioux. Signed by Monlori, White Bear; Waskaijingo, Little Dish; Padamape, Pania-Sticker; Chaponge, Musquitoe; Mindalonga, Partisan or War Chief; Weopaatowechashla, Sun Set; Tokaymhominee, Rock that Turns; Keonorunco, Last Flyer; Mazo, The Iron; Haiwongeeda, One Horn; Mazehaio, Arrow Sender.

(In each of the above four treaties made with various bands of the Sioux, the Indian agent named is one Thomas Forsyth. Interpreters were John A. Cameron, Louis Deconagne, F. Duchonquet, Louis Bufait, J. Bts. Chandonnai, Louis Dorion, Jacques Matte, and John Hay. The wording of each of these four treaties is the

nnme. All promised mutual peace, mutual protection,
and eternal friendship.)

June 1, 1816, a Treaty of peace and friendship, signed
with the eight bands of the Sioux, composing the three tribes
called the Sioux of the Leaf, the Sioux of the Broad Leaf, and
the Sioux who Shoot in the Pine Tops. This treaty, while it
contained the articles concerning "peace and friendship" between the United States as a nation and the Sioux as nations,
also contained an additional article, which provided that the
tribes "confirm to the United States all and every cession or
cessions, of land heretofore made by their tribes to the British, French, or Spanish government, within the limits of the
United States or their territories." It was signed by 41 representatives of the eight bands of the three tribes.

June 22, 1825, Treaty with the Teton, Yancton and Yanc-
tonies bands of Sioux Indians. Provided that all trade and intercourse with the bands shall be transacted at such place or
places as may be designated and pointed out by the President
of the United States, shall be admitted to trade or hold intercourse with said bands of Indians. The three bands promised to
give safe conduct to authorized agents, and to restrict those
who were not authorized. Other conditions of the treaty included
a promise that the Indians would not supply other tribes with
guns or ammunition, and that both the United States and the
three bands would apprehend and deliver to the other, persons
accused of stealing.

July 5, 1825, Treaty with the Sioux and Oglalla bands of
the Sioux tribe of Indians, the same treaty as was signed with
the three bands of Sioux Indians as noted above. Signed at the
mouth of the Teton river.

July 16, 1825, Treaty with the Hunkpapa band of the
Sioux tribe. The same treaty as was signed with the other
Sioux bands in the same year, at the Auricara Village.

August 19, 1825, Treaty with "the Sioux and Chippewa,
Sacs and Fox, Menominee, Ioway, Sioux Winnebago and part
of the Ottawa, Chippewa and Potawattomie tribes all on the
Illinois, at Prairie des Chiens, in the Territory of Michigan.
This treaty provided that "there shall be a firm and perpetual
peace between the Sioux and Chippewas; between the Sioux

and the confederated tribes of Sacs and Foxes; and between the Ioways and the Sioux. Purpose of the treaty, as expressed in its language, was a fear of wars between the tribes, "which if not terminated, may extend to the other tribes, and involve the Indians upon the Missouri, the Mississippi, and the Lakes in general hostilities." The treaty was supposed to "establish boundaries among them and the other tribes who live in their vicinity."

In this treaty, only part of the boundaries were agreed upon. In addition, the chiefs of all the tribes represented agreed "cheerfully to allow a reciprocal right of hunting on the lands of one another, permission being first asked and obtained, as before provided for."

July 15, 1830, Treaty with the Confederated Tribes of the Sacs and Foxes, the Medawah-Kanton, Wahpacoota, Wahpeton and Sisseton Bands or Tribes of Sioux, the Omahas, Ioways, Otoes and Missouries.

In this treaty, the Medaway-Kanton, Wahpacoota, Wahpeton and Sisseton Bands of the Sioux ceded and relinquished to the United States "forever," a tract of country twenty miles in width, from the Mississippi to the Demoine river, situated north and adjoining the line mentioned in the preceding article. The United States agreed "to pay" to the other tribes mentioned in the treaty, certain amounts of money. To the "Sioux of the Mississippi $2,000; to the Yancton and Santie Bands of Sioux $3,000." The United States also agreed to supply the Sioux one blacksmith at the expense of the federal government, "also instruments for agricultural purposes, and iron and steel to the amount of seven hundred dollars."

The United States also agreed to set aside $3,000 annually for ten successive years, to be applied in the discretion of the President of the United States, to the education of the children of the said tribes and bands. The land described in this treaty was originally set aside for the Otoes. Therefore the treaty stipulated that the Sioux and other tribes pay to the Otoes $300 a year for ten years. Provision was also made that "half-breeds" shall be allowed land just as other Indians were allowed. The Treaty was signed at Prairie du Chien, in the Territory of Michigan.

September 10, 1836, Treaty signed between Col Zachary Taylor, then Indian agent, and the Sioux of Wahashaw. The

Indians in this treaty "ceded, relinquished" and quit claimed to the United States all our right, title and interest of whatsoever nature in, and to the lands lying between the State of Missouri and the Missouri river, and do freely and fully exonerate the United States from any guarantee, condition or limitation, expressed or implied under the treaty of Prairie de Chien aforesaid or otherwise, as to the entire and absolute disposition of the said lands, fully authorizing the United States to do with the same whatever shall seem expedient or necessary."

This treaty was forced upon the Sioux under the excuse that it was "desirable that the lands lying between the state of Missouri and the Missouri river should be attached to and become a part of said state, and the Indian title thereto be extinguished . . ." The Indians agreed in the wording of the treaty that "from the local position of the lands in question that they can never be made available for Indian purposes, and that an attempt to place an Indian population on them must inevitably lead to collisions with the citizens of the United States . . ."

The United States agreed, "as a proof of continued friendship and liberality, to give the tribes "presents in the amount of $400, in goods or in money." This infamous document was signed by Sautabesay, (Wabashaw's son); and by Waukauhendeeoatah, Nautaysahpah, Maukpeeaucatpaun, and Hooyah.

October 15, 1836, Treaty with the Yankton and Santee Band of Sioux, and with the Otoes, Missouries, Omahas. Reference is made to the Treaty of Prairie du Chien, July 15, 1830. The Indians now give up their title to lands "lying between the state of Missouri and the Missouri river, and south of a line running due west from the northwest corner of said state until said line strikes the Missouri river." To the Sioux, for their trouble, there was promised $4,520 in presents. This treaty was signed at Bellevue, Upper Missouri.

November 30, 1836, Treaty with the Wahpaakootah, Sisseton and Upper Medawakanton tribes of Sioux Indians. In this treaty as well, the Sioux gave up their right to lands lying between the state of Missouri and the Missouri river. They were promised presents, *in goods*, in the amount of $550.

September 29, 1837, Treaty with "the Sioux Nation of Indians," at Washington, D.C. The Sioux cede "all their land, east of the Mississippi river, and all their islands in the said river." Under this treaty the United States promised to "invest $300,000 in stocks for the Sioux, paying them "annually, forever, an income of not less than five percent. Relatives and friends of the chiefs and braves were to get $110,000. The sum of $90,000 was to be applied "to the just debts of the Sioux." The chiefs and braves were to get an annuity for twenty years of $10,000 in goods. Additionally, the chiefs and braves were to receive $6,000 in goods. While in past treaties, there was provision made for ratification of the treaty by the adult male population authorized to vote, this condition was absent in the 1837 treaty. But ratification by the United States was required.

October 21, 1837, the Yankton Sioux ceded to the United States "all the right and interest in the land ceded by the treaty" of July 15, 1830.

July 23, 1851, Treaty with the Sisseton and Wahpeton Bands of the Sioux. The Sioux "agree to cede, and do hereby cede, sell, and relinquish to the United States, all their lands in the state of Iowa; and also all their lands in the Territory of Minnesota, lying east of the following line: Beginning at the junction of the Buffalo river with the Red river of the North; thence along the western bank of said Red river of the North, to the mouth of the Sioux Wood river; thence along the western shore of said lake, to the southern extremity thereof; thence in a direct line, to the junction of Kampeska Lake with the Tchankasandata, or Sioux river; thence along the western bank of said river to its point of intersection with the northern line of the state of Iowa, including all the islands in the said rivers and lake."

This treaty was signed at Traverse des Sioux, Territory of Minnesota, In a supplemental article, the United States agreed to pay the Sioux ten cents per acre for the lands included in the reservation provided for in the third article of the treaty as originally agreed upon. It was stipulated originally that the following land should be set aside for the Sioux: "all that tract of country on either side of the Minnesota river, from the western boundary of the lands herein ceded, east, to the Tchaytambay river on the north, and to Yellow Medicine river on the south side, to extend, on each side, a distance of not less than ten miles from the general course of said river . . ." This was stricken from the original treaty, and instead the United States promised to make payment "in lieu of such reservation, the amount to be determined later, and to be added to the trust fund of the tribe."

The same supplemental article promised that the President would set aside "such tracts of land as may be satisfactory for their future occupancy and home," but the President was allowed to "vary the conditions."

August 5, 1851. A similar treaty was made with the Mdewakanton and Wahpakoota Bands of the Sioux, they giving up "all their lands and all their right, title and claim to any lands whatever, in the Territory of Minnesota, or in the state of Iowa. Varying amounts of money, and "educational" funds were to be given to the Sioux.

September 17, 1851, Treaty of Fort Laramie with the Sioux or Dahkotahs, Cheyennes, Arapahoes, Crows, Assinaboines, Gros-Ventre Mandans, and Arikaras residing south of the Missouri river, east of the Rocky mountains and north of the lines of Texas and New Mexico.

In this treaty, various territories were assigned for the tribes involved in the conditions of the treaty. The Dahkotahs were promised this land: "commencing the mouth of the White Earth River, on the Missouri river; thence in a southwesterly direction to the forks of the Platte river; thence up the north fork of the Platte river to a point known as the Red Butte, or where the road leaves the river; thence along the range of mountains known as the Black hills, to the headwaters of Heart river to its mouth; and thence down the Missouri river to the place of beginning."

A stipulation stated that it was to be "understood, that, in making this recognition and acknowledgement, the aforesaid Indian nations do not hereby abandon or prejudice any rights or claims they may have to other lands; and further, that they do not surrender the privilege of hunting, fishing or passing over any of the tracts of country heretofore described." This kind of condition was soon to be abandoned.

April 19, 1858, Treaty with the Yankton Sioux, in which they ceded to the United States "all the lands now owned, possessed or claimed by them, wherever situated, except four hundred thousand acres," and all the islands of the Missouri river. The Yanktons agreed to allow the United States free entry through their reservation, and were promised money when they removed to their new reservation, as well as "free and unrestricted use of the red pipestone quarry," held sacred by the Sioux Nation.

June 19, 1858. Treaty with the Sioux Bands of Mendawakanton and Wahpahoota, signed at Washington, D.C. This treaty was perhaps the most restrictive of any thus far negotiated by force with the Sioux. It provided that eighty acres of reservation land be allotted to each head of a family. This was an effort to break up the tribal society.

Land set apart for the tribe in a treaty of August 5, 1851, comprising ten miles on either side of the Minnesota river, was struck out in provisions of this treaty. The Sioux complained that land promised to them was in fact not permitted, and the treaty stipulates that the final decision must be the prerogative of the United States Senate, with a provision that the Senate may decide to sell the Sioux land, giving the "chiefs and headmen" the right to "authorize to be paid out of the proceeds of said tract, such sum or sums as may be found necessary and proper, not exceeding seventy thousand dollars, *to satisfy their just debts and obligations.*" This sum was to be approved by the Secretary of the Interior, to be determined by the superintendent of Indian affairs for the northern superintendency.

The Secretary of the Interior was given additional powers to determine the manner and means of payment of amounts for specific purposes, thus amending the original provision of a former treaty.

June 19, 1858, Treaty with Sisseton and Wahpaton Bands of the Dakotas or Sioux. The treaty of July 23, 1851 was amended, to give each head of a family eighty acres of land, as an allotment. The refusal of the Senate to include a part of the treaty of July 23, 1851, giving the Sioux certain lands, was confirmed in this treaty. In this treaty also, the Sioux were "permitted to use part of the money out of their lands sold," to pay their debts. However, the debts were determined by the United States, the Secretary of the Interior and the government agents. The Secretary of the Interior was again given "discretionary power" as to the manner and objects of expenditures.

NOTE: By the first section of the Act of February 10, 1863, 12th Statutes at Large, page 652, it is provided that: All treaties heretofore made and entered into by the Sisseton, Wahpaton, Medawakanton, and Wahpakoota bands of Sioux or Dakota Indians, or any of them, with the United States, are hereby declared to be abrogated and annulled, so far as said treaties or any of them purport to impose any future obligation on the United States, and all lands and rights of occupancy within the state of Minnesota, and all annuities and claims heretofore accorded to said Indians, or any of them, to be forfeited to the United States.

As an after-measure to the infamous treaty of 1858, the Senate on June 27, 1860, passed a resolution concerning the right and title of certain bands of Sioux Indians, to the lands embraced in reservations on the Minnesota river, and stated that "said Indians possessed a just and valid right and title to said reservations," then allowing them 30 cents an acre for the lands taken.

October 10, 1865, Treaty with the Miniconjou Band of the Sioux, signed at Fort Sully, in the Territory of Dakota. The Miniconjou promised to withdraw from the routes overland already established or to be established through their country. They were promised $20,000 annually for twenty years. The Senate was permitted to amend or modify the treaty, unilaterally, without consultation with the Sioux.

October 14, 1865, Treaty with the Lower Brule Band of the Sioux, signed at Fort Sully, Territory of Dakota. Similar to the one above, except that the Lower Brules were to locate on a permanent reservation at or near the mouth of the White river, to include Fort Lookout, twenty miles in a straight line along the Missouri river and ten miles in depth. This treaty was also made subject to Senate modification or amendment, unilaterally, without approval of the Sioux.

October 19, 1865, Treaty with the Two Kettle Band of the Sioux, signed at Fort Sully, Territory of Dakota. The Sioux also promised, in this treaty, to withdraw from overland routes already established or to be established through their country.

Because soldiers of the United States Army killed Ishtahchah-neaha (Puffing Eyes), chief of the Two Kettles Band, the United States government promised to pay to the surviving widow and her seventeen children the sum of $500, and to the tribe itself as indemnity, a like sum. The Senate was permitted to modify or change the treaty unilaterally.

October 19, 1865, Treaty with the Blackfeet Sioux, made at Fort Sully, Territory of Dakota. As the treaty above, and the Senate had power to unilaterally change or amend the treaty.

October 20, 1865, Treaty with the Sans Arcs Band of the Sioux, at Fort Sully. Same as above.

October 20, 1865, Treaty with the Hunkpapa Band of the Sioux, at Fort Sully. Same as above.

October 20, 1865, Treaty with the Yanktonai Band of the Sioux, at Fort Sully. Same as above.

October 28, 1865, Treaty with the Upper Yanktonai Band of the Sioux, at Fort Sully. Same as above.

October 28, 1865, Treaty with the Oglalla Band of the Sioux, at Fort Sully. Same as above.

February 19, 1867, Treaty with the Sisseton and Wahpeton Sioux at Washington, D.C. This treaty was made with friendly parts of the two bands, numbering 1200 to 1500 persons, who refused to take part in attacking whites who were taking their land; and with another 1,000 to 1200 persons, who refused to take part in the war of the Sioux against the whites in defending their land, but rather fled to the "great prairies of the Northwest, where they still remain." This treaty was made in payment for their services to the United States.

It was recognized that the punitive measures of the government against the Sioux who did take part in the war of defense, were unfortunately extended to the friendly Sisseton and Wahpeton. In payment for their service, the treaty stipulated that "the said bands hereby cede to the United States the right to construct wagon roads, railroads, mail stations, telegraph line, and such other public improvements as the interest of the government shall require, over and across their land." This cession included land previously allowed to them under the treaty of 1851. This was the way the United States repaid the "friendliness."

In consideration of this cession, the government set aside these lands for the Sisseton and Wahpeton: "Beginning at the head of Lake Traverse, thence along the treaty-line of the treaty of 1851 to Kampeska Lake, thence in a direct line to Reipan or the northeast point of the Coteau des Prairies, and thence passing north of Skunk Lake, on the most direct line to the foot of Lake Traverse, and thence along the treaty-line of 1851 to the place of beginning."

Other reservations were set aside for "all other members of the bands who were not sent to the Crow Creek reservation. Also the same conditions were laid down for the Cut Head bands of Yanktonais Sioux. The reservations were to be apportioned in tracts of 160 acres to each head of a family or single person over the age of 21. An agent was placed on the reservation for their control, and certain allocations were made in funds, but only to be used in payment for labor. They also were allowed to trade for furs or peltries within limits of the land of these bands.

Thus were these Sioux bands repaid for their allegiance to the United States government. Their economy was now completely destroyed. They were not allowed to hunt for furs, nor even for their subsistence, but were compelled to an agricultural life, whether or not the land allocated to them was capable of this type of economy. The agricultural implements promised were not given.

The foregoing treaties made with the Sioux, either separately as a tribe, or with individual or combined tribes and bands, actually whittled down their land base with each stroke of the pen. Soon they were destitute. And soon they were fighting against famine, for their very lives, as well as for their reduced lands.

The importance of the Treaty listed hereafter, is therefore, not to be underestimated. It is upon this treaty that modern movements have been founded by the Native Americans. Signed in 1868, in only three more years the United States would officially cease the making of treaties with the natives of the land.

April 28, 1868, Treaty with the Sioux, the Brule, Oglalla, Miniconjou, Yanktonai, Hunkpapa, Blackfeet, Cuthead, Two Kettle, Sans Arcs and Santee, and Arapaho, signed at Fort Laramie, Dakota Territory.

The United States set aside a still different area of land for the Sioux reservation, and a description is given of the geographical boundaries of the reservation. It was "set apart for the absolute and undisturbed use and occupation of the Indians herein named, and for such other friendly tribes or individual Indians as from time to time they may be willing, with the consent of the United States, to admit amongst them." Each person was to receive 160 acres of tillable land, to begin cultivating the soil as farmers.

The government agreed to construct certain buildings for the use of the tribe and government agencies, as well as a saw mill, a grist mill, with shingle-machine attached. Indians who indicated a desire to commence farming, the head of family, shall "have the privilege to select, in the presence and with the assistance of the agent then in charge, a tract of land within said reservation, not exceeding 320 acres, which tract shall be withdrawn from tribal land, to be held by the individual "as long as he shall continue to cultivate it."

Educational opportunities were offered to children between the ages of six and sixteen. For a period of ten years, the government was to provide a teacher, a blacksmith, farmer, physician, carpenter, engineer, and miller. Individuals were to receive clothing, as well as the sum of $10 for each person for a period of 30 years. They were to receive a cow for each family, oxen and such other items needed to develop a narrow truck garden type of subsistence economy.

In payment for such government largesse, the Indians were to withdraw opposition to the construction of the railroad along the Platte river, westward to the Pacific ocean. They were not to oppose the construction of military posts . . . The United States agreed that the country north of the North Platte river and east of the summits of the Big Horn Mountains "shall be held and considered to be unceded Indian territory."

Finally, this document stipulated that "the execution of this treaty and its ratification by the United States Senate shall have the effect and shall be construed *as abrogating and annulling all treaties and agreements heretofore entered into between the respective parties hereto,* so far as such treaties and agreements obligate the United States to furnish and provide money, clothing or other articles of property to such Indians and bands of Indians as become parties to this treaty, but no further."

Among the Indian signers were Spotted Tail, White Bull, Bad Elk, Black Hawk, Bad Wound, Sitting Bull, High Wolf, American Horse, Little Crow, Bad Hand, Poor Bull, Blue Cloud, Spotted Elk, Yellow Robe, Red Cloud, and other leaders of the Sioux, who were herded up and confronted with the order, to sign or be killed.

Signing for the United States were Lieut.-Gen. W. T. Sherman; Gen. William S. Harney, and other high echelon army officers.

A Treaty ratified by the United States Senate, but strangely never proclaimed by the President, is the following:

September 23, 1805, Treaty with the Sioux, following a conference between the United States of America and the Sioux Nation of Indians. The conference was held between the Sioux and Lieut. Zebelon M. Pike, U.S. Army. The Sioux Nation was to grant the United States "for the purpose of establishing military posts, nine miles square at the mouth of the river St. Croix, also from below the confluence of the Mississippi and St. Peters, up the Mississippi, to include the falls of St. Anthony, extending nine miles on each side of the river." The Sioux Nation grants to the United States, the full sovereignty and power over said districts forever, it was stated. In consideration of the "above grants the United States pay to the Sioux $2,000. The Sioux were permitted, by this treaty to pass, repass, hunt or make other uses of the districts. In addition to the signature of Pike, two Indians signed, according to the records: Le Petit Carbeau, and Way Aga Enogee.

Following the ending of the treaty-making relationship between the United States and the Native Americans, agreements continued to be made. Thus, an agreement with the Sisseton and Wahpeton Bands of the Sioux Indians (the so-called "Friendlies" who refused to fight for their land), was made in 1872, in which the two bands were to cede *additional land* to the United States. The agreement was signed at the Sisseton Agency office, Dakota Territory, Lake Traverse reservation. On May 2, 1873, still another agreement was signed by the

61

Sisseton and Wahpeton Bands, in which still further land was ceded to the United States, the government stating that "said territory, now proposed to be ceded, is no longer available to said Indians for the purposes of the chase, and such value or consideration is essentially necessary in order to enable said bands to cultivate portions of the soil and other pursuits" of husbandry.

Another agreement was signed with "the Sioux of various tribes on October 17, 1882," but this agreement was not ratified by the Senate. In this agreement as well, the Sioux were to cede additional lands, in payment for which certain lands were to be allotted to heads of families, and the United States was to deliver cows, bulls, and other items of husbandry and farming to the Sioux.

The land was taken nevertheless, but the Indians never received the promised items, and were not informed that the Senate had failed to ratify the treaty.

Part V

Extermination
Through Legislation

I N ADDITION TO the treaties made with the Indian Nations, in which the main purpose was to gain more and
more Indian land, the United States government passed legislation from the very beginning of its existence dealing with
Indian affairs. The federal legislation served these purposes:
The laws passed by the Congress served to establish the federal-Indian relationship; they set up a structure within which
this relationship functioned; and in effect they served to dispossess, expropriate, and extinguish Indian title to their lands.
Extermination, whether intended or not, was the result. Despite the protestations of the United States government, that
the "Indians are to be protected in their property and rights,"
what actually occurred was the systematic and deliberate deci-
mation of the Indian peoples and many tribes.

The Act of July 22, 1790 reinforced the United States Constitution, which gives Congress ". . . the power to regulate commerce . . . with the Indian Tribes." The 1790 act as an "Act
to regulate trade and intercourse with the Indian tribes." Both
the Constitution and the Act reinforce the status of the federal-
Indian relationship, and are recognition of the unique and different position of the American Indian in this society. The regu-

lation of trade and commerce with the Indian tribes resulted, in actual practice, in bringing the traders and government supervisory staffers onto Indian land, and in their wake the whole gamut of bribery, stealing of land, corruption of Indian life, and extra-legal assignment of Indian land to non-Indians.

The Act of May 28, 1830 was perhaps the most tragic legislation passed by Congress. This act presumably was to exchange federal lands west of the Mississippi for other lands then held by Indian tribes. The act stated that such exchanges should be voluntary; that payment should be made to individuals for improvements relinquished. Suitable guarantees were to be given to the Indians as to the permanent character of their new homes. The act also stated that, "Provided always, That such lands shall revert to the United States if the Indians become extinct, or abandon the same." The tragedy of the Trail of Tears was the result of this act, and it occurred without legal Indian authorization, and despite the promises made in 1830.

A most infamous piece of legislation, historically renowned because of its effects on Indian life, was the Dawes General Allotment Act of February 8, 1887. This act was sparked by the rapid settlement of the West by nonIndians, and the public demand for legislation making possible the acquisition of Indian lands. The Dawes Act authorized the President to allot tribal lands in designated quantities to reservation Indians. The original act provided for approval of the Indians in the allotment process; the Indians were to make their own selections of land; and certain guarantees were made for the appropriation by Congress for the education and civilization of such tribes. However, the act contained this clause: "If any surplus lands remain after the allotments have been made, the Secretary is authorized to negotiate with the tribe for the purchase of such land by the United States . . ." But amendments to the act soon began. In 1888 the act was amended to "authorize the Secretary of the Interior to accept surrenders of patents by Indian allottees."

The effect of the Dawes Allotment Act was to dispossess the Indians of millions of acres of their land. Well into the Twentieth Century, the Dawes Act, under the guise of "assimilating the Indian," continued to act as general exterminator of the Indian as a race of people with a viable economy.

While a substantive treatment of legislation of this type is not the purpose of this *Reader*, the article which follows is of particular interest in describing the various ways in which the Native Americans were separated from their land.

Indian Allotments
Preceding
The Dawes Act

Paul W. Gates*

To some historians of the West the policy of breaking up Indian reserves by allotting them in severalty seems to have had its origin in the Dawes Act of 1887 when a combination of land-hungry Westerners and impractical Eastern idealists are said to have put this allotment act through Congress. The fact that allotments had been made to Indians in the colonial period, were resorted to increasingly in the early years of nationhood, and long before 1887 had become a regular feature of American policy toward the red men is quite neglected. Many thousands of allotments for more than seventeen million acres had been patented to Indians by 1887.

Allotments and individual reserves, generally of 160 to 640 acres, early appeared in treaties with Indians — granted to chiefs, subchiefs, and other headmen, to traders, agents, missionaries, half-breeds, and other influential people who had a part in wresting from the aborigines surrenders of their land. That the allotments when patented quickly fell into the hands of traders and agents who had written provisions into the treaties providing for them is a clear indication of the purpose

*Paul W. Gates is a professor in the Department of History at Cornell University, Ithaca, New York. This paper was given in 1970 at a symposium in honor of George W. Anderson of the University of Kansas. It was later published as a part of *The Frontier Challenge: Responses to the Trans Mississippi West*, by the University of Kansas. It is reprinted as part of the *Reader* with the permission of the author.

for which they were granted. Individual reserves were also another way of enabling the chiefs and headmen to settle their obligations to traders. Associated with provisions for these reserves were sections requiring that much of the money being paid for the cessions of land should go to John Jacob Astor and his partners in the American Fur Company, Pierre Chouteau, and the firm of W. G. & G. W. Ewing and other trading firms, to satisfy their claims.

The first of a long line of individual reserves or grants appears in a treaty of 1805 made with the Choctaws. This was a reserve of 5,120 acres in southwestern Alabama which was to be conveyed to the two daughters of Samuel Mitchell "by Molly, a Chaktaw woman." It was later partitioned and sold by the Mitchell family. A second reserve of 1,500 acres was to be conveyed to John M'Grew. How threats and bribes were combined to induce compliance may be seen in negotiations involving Andrew Jackson that led to a treaty and a cession of land by the Chickasaws in ·1816. Major Levi Colbert ("beloved chief") and Colonel George Colbert were promised three well located tracts of land on the Tennessee and Tombigbee rivers. These grants were confirmed and later sold back to the United States. Another tract of 640 acres was reserved for John M'Cleish and in 1816 confirmed to him and his heirs. In addition to rations and liquor provided during the negotiations, it was stipulated that in consideration of the conciliatory disposition evinced during the negotiations of this treaty, ten chiefs including Levi Colbert and an interpreter should be paid $150 each in goods or cash and to thirteen military leaders $100 each and to William Colbert should be provided a lifetime annuity of $100. Two years later the Chickasaws again were induced to surrender land, this time in western Tennessee; and in consideration of a "friendly and conciliatory dispostion," twenty-one chiefs including Levi and George Colbert were to be given $100 or $150 each.

In two treaties of 1817 and 1819 with the Cherokees—who were under the greatest pressure to remove west of the Mississippi, as were all the Five Civilized Tribes—the allotment plan and cession of land in trust were resorted to. These were to become the means of extensive abuses in the future. These allotments and trust lands were never to become a part of the public domain and subject to the land laws. Every Cherokee head of a family who might wish to become a citizen was to be given an allotment of 640 acres to include his improvements "in which they will have a life estate with a reversion in fee simple to their children." In the event of the allottees' removal, their lands were to revert to the United States. Grants in fee simple of 640 acres were made to thirty-eight named persons, and one grant of 1,280 acres was made to Major John Walker. Some ninety thousand acres in Alabama were ceded "in trust for the Cherokee nation as a school fund."

The difficulties into which the federal officials fell in trying to administer the individual reserves and allotments provided for in the Cherokee treaty of 1819 scarcely argued for a continuation of this practice. Some 311 Indians accepted allotments, but neither Georgia nor North Carolina would concede the right of the federal government to convey them, and instead, compensation had to be given the Indians in the Treaty of New Echota of 1835, by which the Cherokees ceded all their tribal lands remaining in Alabama, Georgia, Tennessee, and North Carolina. In return, they received a fee title to seven million acres in present Oklahoma, $5 million for the surrender of their land and $600,000 to pay for allotments denied them, for other claims, and for the cost of migrating to their new reserve.

The Choctaws were the next of the Civilized Tribes to give way before the inexorable pressure of the settlers intruding into their lands, the states extending their jurisdiction over them, and the federal officials threatening, cajoling, bribing, and dividing them into conflicting groups. In return for the cession in 1820 of a choice tract of west-central Mississippi, including a portion of the Yazoo Delta, a tract of equal size in present western Arkansas was promised, and a blanket, kettle, rifle gun, bullet moulds and nippers, and ammunition sufficient for hunting and defense for one year were given to each member who would emigrate. Also 145,920 acres were to be sold for the benefit of Indian schools. Members of the tribe who had made settlements within the surrendered area and wished to remain on them were each to have 640 acres surrounding their homes. Members preferring to move from their improved land were to be paid its full value.

It soon appeared that the Arkansas tract had already been taken up in part by settlers, and in 1825 the Choctaws again had to go through the same dreary charade of being urged, bribed, or compelled to surrender a tract for the promise of another in the West. Federal officials, including John C. Calhoun, are described as systematically corrupting and intoxicating the Indians during the negotiations leading to the treaty of 1825. Those Indians who preferred to remain on their 640-acre allotments were given the right to sell them in fee simple with the approval of the President. Previously inalienable allotments were opened to sale, subject to the consent of an officer of the government. This was the route most later allotments were to take.

Land-hungry Mississippians were not satisfied by the slow removal of the Indians and the long withholding of parts of the state from settlement. To speed the migration of the Indians, the state extended its laws to persons and property within the remaining reserves, thereby compelling the United States to take more drastic steps against the unwilling natives. A treaty forced upon the Choctaws at Dancing Rabbit Creek in 1830 by systematic bullying by Secretary of War Eaton provided for a new country for them west of Arkansas Territory to which they were given title in fee simple in exchange for another huge cession in central Mississippi and Alabama.

The Choctaws were rashly promised that "no Territory or State shall ever have a right to pass laws for the Government of the Choctaw Nation . . . , and that no part of the land granted them shall ever be embraced in any Territory or State." Members who preferred to remain on their 640-acre allotments east of the Mississippi and who should live on them for five years were to have a fee-simple title. In addition to the 640-acres each head of a family was entitled to, he might have 320 acres for each unmarried child over ten years of age and 160 acres for each dependent child under ten. Finally, 20,420 acres were to be divided among twelve chiefs, and 458,600 acres as cultivation claims were to be allowed to 1,600 heads of families, who were entitled to sell them to the government for fifty cents an acre. One could well say that rarely was the treaty-making power so used to convince the headmen that they could profit by signing personally and quickly, no matter how badly past policies were repudiated. Supplementary articles to the treaty provided for additional allotments amounting to 54,880 acres to named individuals. If the varieties of claims and allotments seems complicated, the management and disposition of the allotments and trust lands involved the government in even more intricate questions.

Negotiations with the Chickasaws in 1832 and 1834 produced treaties whereby the Indians ceded in trust all their lands east of the Mississippi after making allotments of lands to members of the tribe and white men who had cooperated with them. Allotments were to range from 320 acres for orphans to 640 acres for each unmarried person over twenty-one, 1,280 acres for families of two to five persons, 1,920 acres for families of six to ten, and 2,560 acres for families of more than ten. Ownership of one to nine slaves entitled one to 320 acres extra, and for more than ten slaves, 640 acres. The allotments were to be granted in fee simple, but were subject to alienation only with the approval of two chiefs and an officer of the government. In addition to these allotments, four sections each were to be given to "their beloved and faithful old Chief" Levi Colbert and to George and Martin Colbert and three other headmen. Twelve and a half sections were granted other influential Indians and white men.

After the survey of the cession, the selection of the allotments, and special reserves, the remaining lands were to be offered for sale as trust lands and not public domain, at $1.25 an acre. Fearing that combinations of buyers might prevent competitive bidding, as was a common practice at public-land sales, the Chickasaws insisted that no such combination should be permitted without, however, determining how the usual buyers club law could be avoided. Unsold lands continued to be subject to purchase after the auction at $1.25 an acre for a year, when their price was to be reduced to $1.00 an acre; during the next year they could be sold at $.50 an acre, in the fourth year at $.25, and thereafter at $.125. After the deduction of all costs of survey and sale, the income was to be available for the Indians.

The reader will not be surprised to learn that within a short time the bulk of the allotments had passed into the hands of speculating individuals, partnerships, and land companies whose acquisitions ranged as high as 210,658 acres for the American Land Company, 206,787 for the New York and Mississippi Land Company, and 334,602 for Edward Orne, who represented three other land companies. Mary Young found that the first thirty-three buyers acquired ownership of 1,576,-484 acres of allotments. An additional 461,437 acres were sold in amounts of 1,000 to 10,000 acres.

The trust lands were offered in 1836 when 1,304,150 acres were sold for an average of $1.66 an acre. The graduated prices allowed by the treaty brought yearly average prices down to $.18 in 1840 and $.13 in 1850. What is more important, a combination of speculators got much of the land just as they and others had engrossed so many of the allotments. Sixty-one buyers acquired 1,380,311 acres in amounts of 10,000 or more. Buyers whose purchases exceeded 2,000 acres acquired 1,990,-592 acres. Of the 6,718,856-acre cession of Chickasaw lands, at least two-thirds of the allotments and trust lands passed to large buyers. On none of the land were squatters given protection through preemption.

Step by step the Creek Indians, once the possessors of the greater portion of Georgia, surrendered their claim between 1790 and 1827, retaining only a five-million-acre tract west of the Chattahoochee in Alabama. Then in 1832 they, too, were compelled to cede this reserve, but outright, not in trust. However, the treaty provided for ninety full-section reserves to as many principal chiefs and half-section allotments for every head of a family and twenty sections in trust to be sold for the benefit of orphan members of the tribe. Altogether, 2,187,200 acres were allotted. As in other treaties providing for allotments and in accordance with the wishes of the local people, there was no indication that the grants were intended to aid the natives in becoming permanent residents of their tract. Alienation of the allotments was made easier than was the case with individual reserves of other Indians, and there was a scramble by white speculators to buy them. So badly gouged and cheated were the Creeks, despite some slight efforts by the government to assure that a fair price was paid, that it was even proposed to have the allotments bought up by the government and possibly made a part of the public domain. Mary Young lists twenty-four groups and individuals who obtained 1,443,002 acres of Creeks allotments, the largest acquisition being 477,089 acres. Purchasers of 2,000 to 10,000 acres obtained an additional 276,986 acres. The disposal of the allotments to speculating groups brought little return to the Indians as well as great confusion over the right and fairness of the conveyances to the officials involved and surely to the ultimate developers of the land.

North of the Ohio, individual reserves and allotments first appeared in Indian treaties in 1817, setting precedents not easy to overlook in later negotiations. In his instructions to Lewis Cass concerning proposals for discussions with the Indians,

George Graham, Acting Secretary of War suggested that those natives who wished to remain in Ohio might be given "a life estate" in individual reserves "which should descend to his children in fee . . . and that those who do not wish to remain on those terms should have a body of land allotted to them on the west of the Mississippi." Graham added somewhat indiscreetly that there was little expectation that any large cession of land could be obtained for the prices previously paid.

Lewis Cass and Duncan McArthur, the two negotiators who met with the Wyandot, Seneca, Delaware, Shawnee, Potawatomi, Ottawa, and Chippewa tribes, had reason to be apprehensive that they went too far in providing individual reserves and in promising annuities for the cession they secured. In return for the surrender of 3,880,320 acres in northwestern Ohio, northeastern Indiana, and southern Michigan, the tribes were to receive small increases in their annuities. These were slight enough to be considered "unconscionable" by the Indian Claims Commission nearly a century and a half later. The questionable parts of the treaty were the provisions for limited reserves, individual and group, amounting to 271,800 acres, which were to be patented in fee simple with the power of conveying them. In the prose of Cass and McArthur, the persons to whom the reserves were to be given were "almost all . . . Indians by blood." In all cases "it was the urgent wish of the Indians that land should be granted to these persons. To have refused these requests would have embodied against us an interest and created obstacles, which no effort of ours would have defeated or surmounted." It is likely that the traders who expected to gain ownership of the reserves threatened to prevent any cession until the individual reserves were included to the treaty. It was later charged that some of the individual reserves provided for in this treaty and in a treaty with the Chippewas of 1819 were intended for whites who had assumed Indian names and fraudulently claimed Indian children, thus being entitled to consideration. Cass's marked reliance on the word of traders had apparently led him into a serious error.

Congressmen expressed strong doubts about the "unprecedented" privilege of allowing the grantees of individual reserves to sell them to whomever they wished. It was "at variance with the general principles on which intercourse with Indians had been conducted," said the Committee on Public Lands. If alienable reserves were allowed, there would soon be pressure to have reservations allotted to members of the tribes, and the very basis of government policy toward the Indians would be weakened. Secretary of War Calhoun said that the Senate would "probably ratify no treaty which recognizes in the Indian the right of acquiring individual property with the power of selling, except to the United States." Because of the strong opposition of Congress, a second treaty was arranged with the tribes whereby a number of group reservations were enlarged but their status was changed. They were to be held "in the same manner as Indian reservations have been heretofore held," that is as occupancy rights that could only be sold to the government, and individual reserves were made alienable only with the approval of the President. For a time thereafter, a similar restriction was written into other treaties. It came to mean approval by the Office of Indian Affairs, and this, in notable instances, was not difficult to secure. George Graham, Commissioner of the General Land Office, said in 1825 that there was "generally no objection to the Sale of the Lands reserved to Indians," but he thought care should be taken to assure that a fair price was obtained.

Once the importance of including individual reserves in treaties was conceded by the Indian Office, it was found almost impossible to win concessions from the more advanced tribes without them. Such groups were already influenced by and deeply obligated to traders who were turning to land speculations as the fur trade declined. This was notably true of the negotiations with tribes of the Ohio Valley and the border lands of the Great Lakes. Examples are treaties with the Potawatomis, the Weas, and the Delawares in which seventeen individual reserves containing 11,360 acres alienable only with the approval of the President were granted. In a treaty with the Miami tribe of Indiana, whereby a large part of central Indiana and a small tract in Ohio were ceded, there appeared a variation in favor of a chief who was notoriously influenced by traders. Individual Miamis were to be given 31,360 acres of which 25,600 were alienable only with the "approbation of the President," but 5,760 acres, granted to Principal Chief Jean Baptiste Richardville, were conveyed in fee simple without any restriction on alienation. All the reserves were located close to prospective town sites along the Wabash and St. Mary's rivers. In two treaties of 1819 and 1821 with the Saginaw Bay Chippewas and the combined Chippewa, Ottawa, and Potawatomi tribes, by which nearly half the lower peninsula of Michigan was ceded, twenty-one small reserves containing 162,000 acres were withheld and forty-five tracts containing 26,240 acres were assigned to individuals. They were "never to be leased or conveyed by the grantees or their heirs . . . without the permission of the President."

The Chouteau family of St. Louis was long and profitably associated with the Osage Indians, whose claim to land in present Kansas, Missouri, and Arkansas exceeded eighteen million acres. In 1825 the Osages were persuaded to cede some ten million acres of their huge claim, in return for which they were to be paid an annuity of $7,000 in merchandise or money for twenty years and were to be provided with supplies upon ratification. A debt of $1,000 said to be owed to Augustus Chouteau, was to be paid, and forty-two square-mile tracts were reserved for half-breeds, including James G. and Alexander Chouteau. Fifty-four tracts of 640 acres each (34,560) were to be set aside as trust lands and sold for the support of schools for the Osages. In the same year the Kansas Indians agreed that Francois Chouteau was to be paid $500. These were small sums, however, in comparison with those later conceded the Chouteau family and associates.

The Miami treaty of 1826 called for special reserves in Indiana of 17,600 acres of which 2,240 acres were for Jean or John B. Richardville, making his personal ownership 8,000 acres. Other members of the Richardville family received 2,560 acres in the two Miami treaties. Four sections, or 2,560 acres, were assigned to Lagrow, a Miami chief. Seven days after the treaty was signed, it was arranged that the land was to go to John Tipton upon the death of Lagrow. Lagrow died just two months later, and when news of the conveyance to Tipton, who had been the chief person negotiating the treaty, became known, it created a scandal. The validity of the transaction was questioned, but President Jackson seems to have approved it. Eight years later Tipton paid Lagrow's heirs $4,000 for the 2,560 acres to quiet gossip, though probably not to satisfy his conscience. Persons like Tipton were shrewd enough to locate the individual reserves on spots where towns and cities were likely to develop.

Article 7 of the Miami treaty also provided for the purchase by the United States of 6,720 acres which had been granted to individuals in the treaty of 1818. For this acreage

$25,708 was to be paid, or $3.83 an acre. One wonders if these eight-year-old reserves purchased at this price were then sold as public lands at $1.25 an acre.

As Governor of Michigan Territory and Superintendent of Indian Affairs for the Michigan-Indiana area (1813-1831) and later as Secretary of War (1831-1836), Lewis Cass played a leading role in the administration of Indian relations. He had negotiated nineteen Indian treaties and had long since learned that cessions of land could only be obtained if individual reserves were granted and provisions were made for the payment of the Indians' trader debts. In 1826 Cass had a part in drafting the treaties with the Chippewas, the Potawatomis, and the Miamis whereby large tracts of strategically located as well as rich lands suitable for agriculture were surrendered, large sums in money or goods paid, the annuities increased, and many individual reserves granted. In the Chippewa treaty of 1826 the half-breeds were promised section reserves on the St. Mary's River in Michigan. The reserves were to be laid out "in the ancient French manner" of six- to ten-arpents frontage on the river and forty-arpents deep. Also some seventy-seven allotments amounting to 49,280 acres were assigned mostly to the Indian wives and children of white traders and trappers, presumably without power of alienation.

In 1826 the Potawatomis ceded a 130-mile tract bordering the Wabash. To the members of the Burnett family, who had been assigned 5,120 acres in the treaty of 1821, an additional 4,480 acres were now granted. To other chiefs, half-breeds and orphans were given 15,840 acres, and to fifty-eight "scholars in the Carey Mission School" of Isaac McCoy were given 160 acres each. All individual reserves were alienable only with approval of the President.

Cass next negotiated a treaty with the Potawatomis in 1828, which provided eighteen individual reserves totaling 10,240 acres and authorized the purchase of an individual reserve of 640 acres granted by the treaty of 1821 for $1,000. Other treaties that came under Cass's jurisdiction provided for 8,960 acres in individual reserves in Michigan to the Chippewas, Ottawas, and Potawatomis and 26,880 acres of reserves partly in the mineral district of Illinois and Wisconsin to the Winnebagos.

Trust lands appear again in a treaty of 1830 with the Delawares, in which 23,040 acres of "the best land" within a larger cession in southeast Missouri were to be sold to raise a fund for the support of schools,

Although there was strong opposition to granting alienable reserves to full-blooded Indians, except for the Chickasaws, Choctaws, and Creeks of the South, there was less objection at the time to giving reserves to half-breeds. In a treaty of 1830 with the Sac and Fox and three Sioux bands — Omaha, Iowa, and Missouri — two tracts were set aside "to bestow upon half breeds." The tracts were to be held "by the same title, and in the same menner that other Indian Titles are held," but the President was authorized to convey to any of the half-breeds up to 640 acres in fee simple. Because the Sioux half-breeds refused to have anything to do with the 200,000-acre reserve in Minnesota, it was bought back by the United States for $150,000 in 1851. After the allotment of most of the second reserve in Nebraska, the balance of 6,500 acres was sold between 1878 and 1882 for $21,531.

In the Winnebago treaties of 1829 and 1832 wherein large areas in Wisconsin and Illinois were surrendered, 30,720 acres in individual reserves were granted, of which the families of Pierre and John B. Pacquette received 9,600 acres, Catherine Myott received 1,280 acres, and her daughter received 640 acres. One of the elder Myott's sections was conveyed to Henry Gratiot, who signed the treaty in which it had been allowed, and the other was acquired by Nicholas Boilvin, son of a long-time Indian agent at Prairie du Chien. The conveyance of these individual reservations shows that they were floating rights which could be located anywhere within the cession. The Boilvin tract was used to lay out a town. There is no indication that official approval was needed to sell the tracts.

Between 1831 and 1842 the Ohio Indians were divested of title to their remaining lands, amounting to 419,384 acres plus 4,996 acres in Michigan. The Sandusky Senecas, the Senecas and Shawnee of Lewistown, the Shawnee, the Ottawas, and the Wyandots were promised in exchange five reservations containing 449,000 acres in the eastern front of the Indian country to which Eastern tribes were being moved. Since all but the Wyandots held their Ohio reservations in fee, their Kansas reserves were also granted in fee, but the Wyandot reserve was not so granted. Actually, the 109,144-acre tract promised them in 1842 was never turned over to them, and instead they were compelled to buy 23,040 acres at the junction of the Kansas and Missouri rivers from the Delawares for two dollars an acre.

This included the site of present Kansas City, Kansas. In 1850 the Wyandots were paid $185,000 for the reserve they never received, which equalled $1.25 an acre, or all that the United States could hope to derive from the sale of the land.

Three hundred thousand acres of the 419,384 acres thus ceded by the Seneca, Shawnee, Ottawa, and Wyandot Indians were surrendered in trust with the stipulation that they were to be sold to the highest bidder. After the deduction of the costs of survey and sale, the sums advanced to the natives, and $1.25 an acre for the 40,000 acres conveyed by the Sandusky Senecas and $.70 an acre for the other lands, the balance was to be held for the respective tribes.

In the treaty of 1833 with the Ottawas the six Indian grantees were denied the power of alienation without presidential approval; the other grantees presumably were to have that power. By the Wyandot treaty of 1836 seven chiefs were allowed the full price the government received for a section each in the reserve being ceded. Extraordinarily valuable floating rights of 640 acres to be patented in fee simple were granted thirty-five leaders of the tribe by a treaty of 1842. They could be located on "any land west of the Missouri set apart for Indian use, not already claimed or occupied by any person or tribe." Like the better known Valentine scrip of a later time, because of the ease and speed with which it could be laid on prospective town sites, these floats were used by speculators to enter the land on which Lawrence, Emporia, Manhattan, and Topeka were later established.

Altogether there were thirty-two individual reserves granted by these treaties to thirty-seven mixed-bloods, orphans, chiefs, and whites in Ohio for a total of 21,960 acres. All were made alienable sooner or later, including those of Indians. There is little evidence that they remained the property of the grantees for long.

Traders working with the Potawatomi and Miami tribes whose homes were in the Kankakee and upper Wabash valleys succeeded in having the largest quantity of individual and group reserves made in this early period, if we accept the record of allotments made for the Civilized Tribes of Alabama and Mississippi. In the previously cited treaties of 1818, 1826, and 1828 with the Potawatomis, provision was made for 39,840 acres of reserves; and in treaties of 1818 and 1826 with the Miami tribe 45,280 acres were similarly reserved. Treaties of 1832 gave the

Potawatomis an additional 179,200 acres as reserves, making their total, mostly in Indiana, 219,040 acres. The Potawatomis were also promised a reserve in fee simple on the Osage River in the Indian country "sufficient in extent, and adapted to their habits and wants." The ink was scarcely dry on the 1832 treaties with the Potawatomis before the latter were being urged to sell their reserves, and in a series of treaties 97,280 acres were bought for $.62 to $1.25 an acre, or an average of $1.06 an acre. At these rates there was no prospect of the government recovering its investment from the lands; only the traders had profited.

In the drafting of the treaties with the Miami Indians in 1834, 1838, and 1840, when the last of their tribal possessions were surrendered, the practice of making individual reserves reached its most absurd extent. Instructions of July 19, 1833, from the War Department to the agent in charge of negotiations stressed that as many as forty individual reserves could be given, if necessary, and prescribed a top figure of $.50 an acre for a Miami cession. Actually, in the resulting treaty of 1834, only twenty-five individual reserves were granted, but the price paid for the cession was a dollar an acre.

John B. Richardville, principal chief of the Miamis, who already had received 8,000 acres in individual reserves, was given an additional 20,320 acres, and all his holdings were to be conveyed to him in fee. He was also to have $31,800. Francis Godfroy, already the grantee of 4,480 acres, was given 6,400 more and $17,612. The three Miami treaties brought the total reserves granted them to 112,800 acres. A total of $1,133,000 was to be paid for the cessions of these three treaties, a sum far larger than the United States could expect to recover from their sale. The Miami were also promised a reservation in the Indian country of 500,000 acres which was to be guaranteed "to them forever."

So generously paid were the Potawatomi and Miami Indians for their Indiana land that they became among the best-endowed of all Indians. In 1853 the per capita return to the Miamis in the form of annuities and other payments was $87, that of the Eel River Miamis was $68, in both cases exceeding that of all other tribes. The per capita payments of annuities and other grants to the Potawatomis were exceeded by those paid three other tribes (the Sac and Fox of Missouri, the Sac and Fox of Mississippi, and the Winnebagos), but the total

77

paid the Potawatomis, $91,804, was only exceeded by that of the Winnebagos, $97,485.

Some Indian officials were becoming increasingly troubled by the fact that individual reserves were being granted so extensively. It is not clear, however, whether their concern stemmed from knowledge that for the most part the reserves quickly fell into the hands of traders and others exploiting the ignorance of the natives. After Lewis Cass (that warm friend, and some would say pliant tool, of the traders) became Secretary of War, he instructed commissioners to treat with the Potawatomis for cessions of their land in 1833 as follows:

Decline, in the first instances, to grant any reservations either to the Indians or other, and endeavor to prevail upon them all to remove. Should you find this impracticable, and that granting some reservations will be unavoidable, that course may then be taken in the usual manner and upon the usual conditions. But I am very anxious that individual reservations should be circumscribed within the narrowist possible limits. The whites and the half-breeds press upon the Indians, and induce them to ask for these gratuities, to which they have no just pretensions; and for which neither the United States nor the Indians receive any real consideration. The practice, though it has long prevailed, is a bad one and should be avoided as far as possible.

A combination of able and aggressive traders stationed at Fort Wayne and Logansport, Indiana, who worked at times closely with Senator John Tipton, completely ignored all such instructions in securing cessions from the Miami and Potawatomi Indians without any sharp disapproval from Cass, but elsewhere in the upper Mississippi Valley individual reserves were halted or kept to a minimum.

The government's reluctance to grant individual reserves is best displayed in the negotiations for three treaties with the combined Chippewa, Ottawa, and Potawatomi Indians of 1833 and with the Ottawas and Chippewas of 1836, whereby some five million acres in Illinois and Wisconsin and from one-third to one-half of Michigan were surrendered to the United States. It was found that the traders who had close relations with these Indians and whose support was essential could be satisfied if provisions were included in the treaties for the payment of the debts of the Indians, real or imaginary, and sums of money equivalent to what the traders might have expected to get from individual reserves. Both these conditions were well met. In the two treaties with the combined tribes $100,000 was provided for "sundry individuals, in behalf of whom reservations were asked, which the Commissioners refused to grant." One hundred and fifty thousand dollars was provided to satisfy the claims of traders and $600,000 for miscellaneous purposes, including an annuity. Three lists of claimants and persons to whom the tribes wished to grant favors were included in the treaty, in all 351 individuals, groups, or companies, some of which were listed for multiple claims. Milo M. Quaife, historian of Chicago, speaks of "the striking display of greed and dishonesty" of many of those who strove to have doubtful claims included. Largest of the claims were those of the American Fur Company ($20,300) and of members of the Kinzie family ($23,216), who had previously had $7,485 paid them under treaties of 1828 and 1829. Many of the payments were for claims that Quaife thinks should rightly have been assumed by the United States, not by the Indians. He expressed surprise that numerous beneficiaries on the three lists signed the treaties, being apparently unaware that government negotiators had long worked with and through traders who received direct and indirect boons from the treaties, which they had aided in extorting from the natives and which they had signed as witnesses. The combined tribes were given a reservation of five million acres in western Iowa in exchange for their lands in Illinois, Wisconsin, and Michigan.

During the negotiations leading to a treaty of 1836 with the combined Ottawa and Chippewa, the traders demanded individual reserves and inclusion in the treaties of specific provisions for the payment of stipulated claims. Rix Robinson, agent of the American Fur Company, was heavily in debt to the company, and the only way he could square his obligations was to get them paid by the Indians. Ramsay Crooks of the American Fur Company in his numerous instructions to Robinson, who was with the Indians throughout the discussions leading to the treaty, continually emphasized that payment for Robinson's claim must be included in any treaty of cession. Individual reserves, with their chances of hidden profits, were much wanted, and the tribes were anxious to provide them for their half-breeds; but "the President having determined" not to allow any, it was agreed that $300,000 was to be allowed for the payment of debts, $150,000 should be divided among the half-breeds, and $48,180 should be paid the half-breed children of traders in place of 19,040 acres of individual reserves, previously assigned. Included in the latter was the sum of $23,040 for the family of Rix Robinson, most of which, if not all, went to the American Fur Company. Another claim of $5,600 was included for an employee of the company and his family. The employee had become blind, and Crooks used his influence to get a position for him as an interpreter and aid for other members of his family, thereby passing the burden to the government.

Michigan Chippewas were denied the right to assign individual reserves but were allowed to cede 107,720 acres in trust in 1836 and 1837 with a stipulation that specifically exempted this land from preemption. Because the Indians feared that a combination of purchasers would prevent them from getting the actual value of their land when sold at auction, it was stipulated that for the first two years they were to be sold at no less than $5 an acre and any land remaining thereafter was to be held at $2.50. After five years, remnants of the land could be sold at $.75.

Floating reserves, free to be located within broad areas or whose boundaries were not clearly defined, were much sought after by speculators, as were also reserves specifically located on sites almost certain to be valuable for town locations. In 1825 twenty-seven Kansas half-breeds were assigned full-section reserves on the north side of the Kansas River, which became the object of much intrigue by speculators because of their choice location. Similarly, we have seen how the Wyandot floats of 640 acres each were in great demand because of the priority given them in the selection and entry of land. One unusual reserve was included in a treaty of 1835 with the Caddo Indians of Louisiana, unusual because of its size and because individual reserves were not common in Louisiana or Arkansas. The reserve was for four square leagues—23,040 acres. The grantee, Francois Grappe, a black man, had never been known to have any interest in this land, though it was later estimated to be as much as 34,500 acres because of the way it was blocked out. It was laid on rich alluvial soil bordering the Red River and was subsequently estimated to be worth somewhere between $100,000 and $900,000. The basis for the reserve was an alleged donation of the land by the Indians some thirty-four years earlier. After ratification of the treaty and the approval of the patent, accusations of gross fraud led to a congressional investigation which in 1841 brought out the fact that the tract had been acquired by the commissioner in charge of negotiating the treaty and that in all likelihood arrangements for the purchase from Grappe had been made beforehand. Witnesses also testified that the tract had been improved by white planters, who had a good title dating back to the Spanish period, and furthermore that it was not a part of the Caddo reservation and that the Indians had no right to include it in their cession. The House Committee on Indian Affairs considered the conduct of the commissioner "unfortunate" and "highly imprudent," scored the testimony in his behalf as utterly worthless, deplored the many fabrications of documents, and was deeply troubled by evidence that the commissioner had not only abused the treaty-making power and suppressed evidence contrary to his interest but had also grossly cheated the Indians in the rations and supplies the government had intended for them. The committee concluded that the district attorney should bring suit to recover the tract, which it declared had been "improperly or fraudulently" included in the treaty. There was a close parallel between the Caddo fraud and the Lagrow reserve which John Tipton had acquired. One may well wonder how Cass could have favored, or the Senate ratified, the Caddo reserve, the largest included in any of the treaties in a period in which reserves were being frowned upon.

One may conclude that thus far, individual reserves to chiefs, orphans, Indian children of white traders, and political hangers-on were not planned with any real thought of enabling the Indians to move from communal or tribal ownership. Instead, they were used in the South as a means of eliminating the Indians by giving them property whose value and use they had no conception of other than as a means to a few drinks. The authors of the allotment policies in the treaties with the Creeks, Choctaws, Chickasaws, and Cherokees were aware that the lands would shortly be in the possession of whites. In the North, the individual reserves offered a means by which the support of traders could be obtained for cessions of land and the removal of the Indians, which would mean the end of their profitable business with the natives. Also, the reserves and stipulations for payment of debts in the treaties would permit the chiefs and headmen to rid themselves of those obligations that the traders had permitted, if they had not actually encouraged, them to accumulate. If the debts were listed in the treaties and it was stipulated that they were to be paid out of the large sums authorized for this purchase, the traders were sure of collecting. Few of the treaties did so list the sums to be paid, but those that did are useful in showing how business was conducted with the Indians and the way in which they were exploited.

Largest of the traders' claims to be paid was that of $133,997 to Pratt, Chouteau & Co., and members of the prolific Chouteau family. Second largest was the $76,587 paid to the firm of W. G. & G. W. Ewing and family. It was G. W. Ewing who informed Senator Tipton of Indiana that the Potawatomi Indians would never leave the Wabash until his firm was paid the full debt owed it. The third largest of the sums paid for Indian debts went to John Jacob Astor and the American Fur Company, $59,961. Actually, the total received by the Astor-American Fur Company was far larger, for they had a major share in the Pratte, Chouteau & Co.; $20,961 assigned to others in the Chicago treaty of 1829 was collected by Astor, and other sums appearing under other names were either for Astor or for the company. G. W. Ewing also had at least $37,000 of claims confirmed in addition to those included in treaties.

The *Wisconsin Herald* of September 27, 1845, a paper published in Prairie du Chien, where more gold and silver was distributed in the form of annuities to Indians than in any other place north of St. Louis, described the scramble by whites to get their hands on the funds being paid the Indians:

> Everybody claimed kin with the Indians and could bring proof of his genealogy about annuity day. How this money was watched all the way from Washington. Speculators, sharpers, gamblers and knaves followed it, and were in Prairie du Chien thick as buzzards when the annuities were to be paid. Princely was the sum disbursed, but thousands . . . stood eager to share it, and the money passed away like the dew.

By 1853 the Indians had surrendered their lands east of the Mississippi and in the first tier of states west of that river with the exception of northern Minnesota and small reservations elsewhere and had moved to the Indian country west of

Missouri and Arkansas. In 1844, 85,473 tribesmen lived in the Indian country, much the larger number being in the region west of Arkansas. In 1854, 8,002 intruded Indians were reported in Kansas. There, on clearly defined reservations they dwelt in misery, partly sustained by inadequate government aid and denied the freedom from white intrusions that their treaties had guaranteed them. Westward-moving Mormon refugees seeking relief from religious persecution, pioneers and traders looking for new opportunities in Oregon and New Mexico, and the rush of gold seekers to California in 1849 meant new trouble for the intruded Indians, as did the demand for their removal from the better lands in the Nebraska Territory that had been promised them in perpetuity.

The induced or forced migration of Eastern tribes to the west of the Mississippi began before definite plans for an Indian country had been adopted. Cherokee and Choctaw Indians were assigned reservations in Arkansas, and Delawares and Kickapoos were given tracts in Missouri; but by 1825 the granting of reservations in states or territories was halted. Thereafter, with a few exceptions, Indians were moved into unorganized areas west of Missouri and the Territory of Arkansas.

In 1830 Congressional policy was somewhat crystalized by an act of May 28, which restricted removals to areas that were not included in a state or organized territory but for which the Indian title had been extinguished. This effectively defined the Indian country of present Oklahoma, eastern Kansas, and southeastern Nebraska and Iowa and Minnesota. To induce the Indians to give up their more eastern reserves, the President was authorized solemnly to assure them that "the United States will forever secure and guarantee to them, . . . the country so exchanged . . . and if they prefer it . . . will cause a patent of grant to be made and executed to them for the same." Then followed negotiations with the Senecas and Shawnees; the Kickapoos; the federated Kaskaskia, Peorias, Piankeshaws, and Weas; the Iowas, the Chippewas, and Wyandots, which provided for their removal across the Missouri line; and with the Creeks, Choctaws, Seminoles, Chickasaws, and the Seneca-Shawnees for their removal to reservations in what was to become Indian Territory.

The area west of Arkansas and Missouri contained much first-rate arable land that was suitable for grain and livestock production and capable of sustaining a large population. By

1850 many Westerners had come to the conclusion that an earlier generation had made a major error in designating the region permanent Indian country.

All of Indian Territory, except the panhandle, and the entire front of Kansas were in the possession of some 85,000 intruded Indians. They had been promised their reservations "in full and complete possession . . . as their land and home forever." What then was the prospect of creating new territories and states out of the Indian country? Congressmen knew the way and proceeded to follow it. First, in 1853 they added to the annual appropriation bill for the Office of Indian Affairs a section authorizing the Commissioner of Indian Affairs to negotiate with the Indians west of Missouri and Iowa for the extinguishment of their titles "in whole or in part" and appropriated $50,000 to further that end. Meeting no favorable response, the Commissioner had to report failure in his first effort. Notwithstanding this failure and its plighted word, Congress next adopted the Kansas-Nebraska Act on May 30, 1854, for the creation of two territories and the opening of them to settlement. True, the rights of the Indians were to be preserved, and their reservations were excluded from the territories "until the tribes gave their assent" to such inclusion.

The passage of the Kansas-Nebraska Act was the signal for thousands of land-hungry people, looking for the economic opportunities that new territories provided, to rush across the Missouri line into Kansas. They disregarded Indian ownership, marked out their claims, built improvements that would justify preempting the land, established local government and put it into operation. The carpetbag officials whom the Pierce administration sent in to "rule" and officers of the Army united with the land seekers to break down the morale of the Indians and compel them to remove. Officers at Fort Leavenworth permitted the creation of a town on the Delaware lands and participated in the speculation without making any protest, though all was contrary to law. This lawless example led hundreds of Missourians to penetrate into the Delaware tract and into other reservations, disregarding the admonishments and warnings of Indian officials. The territorial governor took up office on Indian lands, and the legislature authorized polling places and held its session on Shawnee lands and extended county organization over some reservations, all in violation of the treaties and the territory's organic act. Protests to the Secretary of War and to the President were all to no avail; no one save the Indian Commissioner paid any attention to the rights guaranteed the Indians, and he was later to be displaced by a commissioner who was more sympathetic to Western attitudes.

Everywhere "trespass and depredations of every conceivable kind" were committed against the Indians. They were "personally maltreated, their property stolen, their timber destroyed," and all their rights jeopardized. There seemed no alternative to surrender and removal.

In the twenty-four days before Franklin Pierce signed the Kansas-Nebraska Act, the Commissioner of Indian Affairs had wrested from the reluctant Indians along the eastern border of the Indian country six treaties surrendering portions of their reserves in trust and portions outright, and providing that other parts were either to be retained in tribal ownerships for a time or were to be distributed in allotments to chiefs, headmen, heads of families, and half-breeds. The swarms of land seekers that swept across the Missouri border found no public lands in easy reach but met up with Indian trust lands, allotments, floating allotments, diminished reserves, and reserves still intact. On all of these lands settlement or intrusion by whites was illegal. The conflicts that emerged between the Indian occupants and owners on the one side and the intruders on the other, and the desperate struggles between contending whites for town sites, railroad terminals, county seats, the territorial capital, and land claims I have discussed as a major theme in the Kansas conflict in *Fifty Million Acres: Conflicts over Kansas Land Policy, 1854-1890.*

A summary of the management and disposal of the Kansas Indian lands shows that few tracts in eastern and southern Kansas ever became a part of the public domain but instead were either alloted (at least 525,000 acres) or sold in trust for the benefit of the Indians (10,888,000 acres). On none of this land was homestead to apply, nor could military warrants with their reduction in cost to settlers be accepted for entries. To this extent had Congress permitted setting aside the public-land laws for most of eastern and southern Kansas.

The inclusion of allotments to chiefs, heads of families, and half-breeds had shown land-hungry elements how to hasten the opening of Indian lands and overcome the reluctance of the natives to surrendering their tribal reserves. With the opening of Kansas and Nebraska territories the allotment of Indian lands in severalty became a regular feature of the treaties being negotiated with tribes in the two new territories and in Minnesota, Oregon, Dakota, Colorado, Utah, Montana, Arizona, Idaho, and Wyoming territories and in Michigan. In the seven years following 1854, forty treaties included provisions for surveying the reservations and alloting the lands to individual Indians in amounts from 80 to 320 acres. Fourteen of the treaties applied to Kansas tribes, five to Washington tribes, and smaller numbers to tribes in other territories. In 1867 Indian commissioners included in treaties provisions allowing patents of 160 acres to Indians who had 50 acres fenced, plowed, and in crops (Sisseton and Wahpeton Sioux) or patents to each 40 acres of which 10 acres were cultivated, up to 160 acres (Chippewa of Minnesota). Provisions for assigning land to interested Indians, issuing certificates showing their exclusive possession, and for listing the certificates in the land books of the tribes were included in treaties with the Cheyenne and Arapaho, the Crow, the Sioux, the Navajo, the Shoshone, and the Ute Indians in 1867 and 1868.

Indians in Michigan, Wisconsin, Minnesota, Nebraska, and Kansas were either given alienable titles or titles that could be and were made alienable by officials of the Department of the Interior, but the treaties with the "wild" Indians farther west offered no promise of alienation short of twenty-five years. In these latter cases the title in the allotments was only possessory and could only be conveyed to the United States or to the tribe, or in the event of disease of the allottee, his right could pass on to heirs though it remained inalienable. It was less possible for officials to speed the process of patenting these allotments, as they had done so extensively with allotments in Kansas, Indiana, and Michigan; and these allotments were not subject to taxation, mortgage, or lease.

Commissioners of Indian Affairs Manypenny, in 1855, Dole, in 1863, and E. P. Smith, in 1873, emphasized allotments as a means of inducing the redmen to make improvements on their tracts and to become farmers. The commissioners regarded the policy as the only one that offered a hope of ending tribal ownership and gradually assimilating the Indians into the acquisitive white culture of the frontier. The Board of Indian Commissioners, which was appointed to scrutinize the operations of the Indian Office and to bring to public attention any mismanagement it uncovered, recommended in its first report in

1870 a general allotment policy. In the words of Angie Debo, it thereafter "regarded the extent of allotment as the measure of progress in Indian advancement." It urged, however, that titles should be inalienable for two or three generations. Carl Schurz, Secretary of the Interior from 1877 to 1881, threw his influence behind allotment, as did Senator Henry L. Dawes and other so-called humanitarians. Yet the evidence that the allotments failed to effect this objective was already clear wherever they had been given. The Kansas story should have been sufficient to deter experimenting with an allotment policy. The record of allotments in Michigan is perhaps less well known.

By treaties of 1855 and 1864 with the Ottawas and Chippewas parts of six townships in Michigan were set aside for allotments of 80 acres each, and some 1,735 Indians were given patents by 1871. E. A. Hayt, Commissioner of Indian Affairs in the Hayes administration, related the sad story of the victimization of the owners despite their relatively advanced state. So certain were the Indians that they would be removed, despite their allotments, that they were disinclined to improve or in any way make use of their land, an attitude expressed in the reports of the Indian Office. A major portion 'fell victims to the greed of unscrupulous white men, and, one by one," parted with or were defrauded of their lands. "Every means that human ingenuity can devise, legal or illegal, has been resorted to for the purpose of obtaining possession" of the lands. Many sold their allotments for as little as $.25 an acre when they were worth $5 to $25 an acre. Collusion between the agents and the purchasers, liberal use of whiskey, the application of unequal taxes, and mortgaging, all contributed to lead the Indians to sign away their rights. In 1875 it was estimated that not one in ten of the allotments was still held by the Indians. Hayt's analysis shows that the Michigan record was almost a duplication of the Kansas frauds of a few years earlier. Ten years later the local agent concluded that giving Indians titles they could convey resulted "in the almost entire dispossession of their land by bartering them away without scarcely any equivalent therefore." He asserted that allotments of the lands and their transfer to whites was part of "a well-laid scheme contemplated many years ago, ripened and consummated openly . . . without the intervention of the Government" whose duty it was to protect the Indians against the wiles of the exploiters "who have grown wealthy by their ill-gotten gains, taken from the people whom they now despise.

At least 11,763 patents for allotments had been issued by 1886, in Kansas, Nebraska, and other states of the Upper Mississippi Valley. This does not include the many thousands given the Creeks, Cherokees, Choctaws, and Chickasaws in Alabama and Mississippi. There was little or nothing in the record of allotments, however, to encourage the belief that they promised a humane and practical solution of the Indian problem. Yet since further concentration of the redmen in Indian Territory and in one or two other large reservations was unacceptable to the West, as Loring Priest has admirably pointed out, allotment was increasingly stressed as the only long-range solution, the more so as the errors of the past were glossed over or forgotten. Former Commissioner Manypenny might well have been listened to in 1885 when he declared that had he been able to foresee how completely the allotment policy would be discredited, "I would be compelled to admit that I had committed a high crime" by pursuing it in Kansas.

Neither Congress nor the authorities in the Indian Office were prepared to oppose the allotment policy when legislation to establish it generally was considered. It is true that the Coeur d'Alene, Yankton Sioux, Potawatomi, Kickapoo, Wyandot, Iowa, and the Five Civilized Tribes had made known their opposition so strongly that the Commissioner mentioned their views in his report, somewhat reluctantly, it appears. Other natives, however, he reported as anxiously awaiting the allotment of their reserves. J. P. Kinney marshaled some evidence showing that Indians domiciled on allotments in New Mexico, Minnesota, Nebraska, and elsewhere were making progress toward independence and full ownership of their tracts; but his information is drawn from the reports of agents who were committed to the policy. In 1883 "over fifty" Santee Sioux were reported to have obtained patents for their allotments; but all such information is from strong supporters of allotments, and no later information is given concerning the retention of ownership once the fee title had passed. Information concerning the progress of allotments among the other Plains tribes before 1887 is not accessible. Most supporters of allotments agreed that extensive experience with them indicated that final ownership should be long delayed, except for those making unusual progress.

Henry Moore Teller, for many years Senator from Colorado,

who commonly reflected Western and particularly Colorado sen timent on most questions, as Secretary of the Interior from 1881 to 1885 favored a different policy toward Indian lands, not, however, because of any humane concern for the Indians, for he callously neglected Indian rights and needs. He was both aware of, and frankly admitted, the fact that the great mass of Indians were violently opposed to allotment, an admission that required some courage at that time. To satisfy the land hunger of the West, Teller favored drastic reduction of the reserves and the opening of the surplus lands to settlers only. At the same time he would give the tribes a fee-simple title to their diminished reserves, which, he thought, would remove from them the fear of the loss of their lands and their consequent unwillingness to develop or in any way improve them. While Teller took a strong stand in opposition to allotment, his Commissioner of Indian Affairs, Hiram Price, supported the allotment policy as strongly as his chief opposed it. He maintained that "the best results" had followed from allotment and declared, "I shall, therefore, adhere to the policy of alloting lands wherever the same can legally be done and the condition of the Indians is such as to warrant it." Like his predecessors in the Indian Office, he reported that many Indians were clamoring for allotments.

Senator Joseph N. Dolph of Oregon was one of the few Western members of Congress who foresaw the evils in the allotment policy. He predicted in 1887, when the measure to provide for forced allotting of Indian lands was under consideration, that they would be swiftly disposed of to whites, the proceeds squandered, and the Indians would not be prepared for self support and would again be dependent on government benevolence.

The West, Congress, the Indian Office, and some of the true friends of the Indians wanted a general allotment act which would require its application to all Indians or to all but those in the Indian Territory, where opposition was intense. Such a combination was too powerful to resist. The Dawes General Allotment Act became law on February 8, 1887. It followed previous measures in the size of allotments and the twenty-five-year period before fee-simple titles could be obtained, and provided for the sale of surplus lands only to actual settlers. Whatever the motives of those who worked for the enactment of the measure, its success in achieving its avowed object—the gradual assimilation of the Indian population—was dependent on sympathetic, honest, and understanding administration; and that the Dawes Act did nothing to assure. One need not wonder why the Act has come in for penetrating criticism in later years in the light of the demoralizing effect its incidence had upon the economy of the Indians.

Part VI

Presidents of the United States in American Indian History

Rupert Costo

T HE UNITED STATES had been an independent nation for 72 years when President Lincoln complained about "this accursed Indian problem." Eighty-five years later, President Hoover said, "A certain amount of the time of every President from George Washington down has had to be devoted to 'Indian Affairs.' Certainly, our 400,000 Indians consume more official attention than any twenty cities of 400,000 people."

The United States of America has been an independent sovereign nation for one hundred and ninety-eight years, and the so-called "Indian question" is still its most profoundly disturbing internal problem. The oldest and biggest federal bureaucracy exists as a huge agency for this purpose. It is called the Bureau of Indian Affairs. The Courts and Congress are occupied continuously with Indian litigation and Indian legislation, and its records constitute a veritable mountain of legal literature.

The fact that the time and efforts, the funds and energies of this government have been preoccupied for nearly two hundred years with Federal-Indian relationships, signifies the extreme failure of the government's policy towards the tribes.

The result has been so unsatisfactory that President Lyndon B. Johnson found it necessary to issue a special appeal to Congress in March, 1968, in which he said, "The most striking fact about the American Indians today is their tragic plight." If nothing else, President Johnson's special message brought to light a fact that few indeed understand. That is, that the Presidents of the United States have always played a far more important role in Indian affairs than is generally recognized. Their role in determining policy, initiating actions, signing or vetoing legislative acts, and in fact deciding the fate of the Indian Tribes, has always been significant and often crucial.

With the advent of the white man upon this continent, both Britain and the United States treated the Indian Tribes as they dealt with independent foreign nations. From September 17, 1778, when George Washington made the first treaty with the Delawares, to August 13, 1868, the United States made 370 treaties with the native tribes. The treaty with the Delawares was one of seven signed under the Continental Congress. The Delawares agreed to "engage to join the troops of the United States . . ." It also proposed to "form a state whereof the Delaware nation shall be the head, and have a representation in Congress." A treaty was made with the Six Nations on October 22, 1784. A second pact was signed with the Delawares on January 31, 1785, which further emphasized the sovereignty of the Indian nations. Article five of this treaty states that any citizen of the United States, or other person shall not attempt to settle on Indian lands, and if he does so, "such person shall forfeit the protection of the United States, and the Indians may punich him as they please . . ." The extent to which recognition was given historically to Indian ownership (not merely *occupation*) of territory upon this continent is seen in the fact that as late as 1796, 1799, and 1802, some of the Trade and Intercourse Acts passed by the United States Congress required that "a citizen or inhabitant of the U.S. to acquire a passport before going into the country secured by treaty to the Indians."

Upon adoption of the Constitution, the United States continued to make treaties with the Indian tribes. This power is vested in the President of the U.S. in Article II, Section 2 of the Constitution, and requires ratification by the Senate. But the power of the President in Indian affairs is not confined to the treaty-making authority. The President was granted powers of superintendency, the making of regulations, and control over many aspects of Indian life. Presidential powers were extended through statutes, in treaties, and in some legislation enacted by Congress. Some treaties provided that the President shall have the power to establish trading posts, military posts, to appoint agents, dispose of certain lands, approve patents, and act in intertribal claims.   When the Bureau of Indian Affairs was placed under the jurisdiction of the Secretary of the Interior in 1849, the powers of the President began to have references in litigation. Thus, in *Wolsey vs. Chapman*, the court determined that the action of the Commissioner of Indian Affairs must be presumed to be the action of the President. In *Maxwell vs. United States*, the court held that the direction of the President is generally presumed, in instructions and orders issuing from competent federal departments.

The office and the person of the President are thus of critical significance, when considering any aspect of Indian affairs. The President's economic interests, his region of origin, culture and philosophy, political debts due on demand by supporters of his election and career, and his personal prejudices, have much to do with his policies in connection with matters concerning the Indian people of the United States.

This article does not propose to consider all these aspects of Presidential influence on Federal-Indian relationships. However, at every turning point in American Indian history, there has always been the Commanding Officer of the United States of America, indicating the direction, forbidding or permitting, enforcing or resisting, and in general representing, not the interests of the Native Americans, but infallibly and unfailingly representing the interests of the predominantly influential and vital economic forces of American society at that point in the history of the nation.

Before the adoption of the Constitution, General George Washington's special task was to win the Indian Nations as allies in the Revolutionary War, or to fight them as enemies on the side of Britain. Washington was well aware of the power of the tribes, to such an extent that he agreed to their request that various tribes be permitted representation in Congress. Even at this early time, the leaders of the new nation envisioned the creation of an Indian State, to which the tribes would be removed, with representation in Congress, of a sort. This was the first, and the least devastating expression of the removal policy. It was short lived.

In July, 1787, the Continental Congress enacted a law which had far-reaching consequences upon the Indian. This was the Northwest Ordinance. That part of the Ordinance which refers to Indian affairs is found in Article 3, which states in part, ". . . The utmost good faith shall always be observed towards the Indians; and in their property rights, and liberty; they shall never be invaded or disturbed, unless in just and lawful wars authorized by Congress; BUT LAWS FOUNDED IN JUSTICE AND HUMANITY SHALL FROM TIME TO TIME BE MADE (emphasis added), for preventing wrongs being done to them, and for preserving peace and friendship with them." This wording has an aura of humanity and justice, certainly. It is a fact, however, that Article 3, as reaffirmed with slight modifications in 1789 by the first Congress under President Washington, was the first official enactment in which Congress legislated Indian affairs with plenary authority. The door was open, and from then on there emanated a mass of statutes, laws, and judicial decisions, all having to do with the conversion of Federal-Indian relations from that of treating with the tribes as independent foreign nations, to the relationship enunciated by Chief Justice Marshall in the 1830's as "domestic DEPENDENT nations," then to the cessation of treaty-making in 1871, and the establishment of reservations "to keep the Indians quiet," with its infamous elements of captivity and rationing.

While the first treaties signed by Washington established peace, and tied the Indian nations to the United States as allies, American troops soon began to occupy and build forts in Indian territory. The Indians resisted. Certain treaties forbid it. In July, 1797, the chiefs of the Ohio Tribes issued a written ultimatum to the United States, that American troops must withdraw to their original boundaries at the Ohio River, in accordance with the terms of the agreement made at Fort Stanwix in 1768. By military action, Washington's General ("Mad Anthony") Wayne then entered the lands of the Ohio Confederacy and waged a merciless battle at Fallen Timbers, which culminated in the Treaty of Greenville. Thus, the United States, by force and unprovoked invasion, acquired the entire state of Ohio and part of Indiana.

The Washington policies continued in force during the administration of John Adams, from 1797 to 1801. Encroachment upon Indian land continued into the administration of President Jefferson, who in 1786 had written of "the sacredness" of Indian rights, stating, "... not a foot of land will ever be taken from the Indians without their consent." But Jefferson is also quoted as having urged that, "In order to facilitate the transfer of Indian lands to the United States, the influential chiefs be encouraged to go into debt because we observe that when these debts get beyond what the individual can pay, they become willing to lop them off by a cession of lands ..."

In 1802, under Jefferson's administration, the infamous Georgia compact was made, in which the federal government agreed "to extinguish Indian title at its own expense ..." in the state of Georgia. The idea of removal of the Indian tribes from their various homelands appears to have originated with Jefferson, who, in 1803, in connection with the Louisiana Purchase, drafted a constitutional amendment which provided for the exchange of Indian lands east of the Mississippi for land in the west, and also for the exchange of lands in the east owned by white settlers, for land in the older portion of the country. Some of the greatest land grabs occurred under his administration.

In a treaty of 1809 with the Delawares, Potawatomies, Miamis, Kickapoos and Eel River Tribes, three million acres of choice land were ceded to the United States along the Wabash River, for $8,200 cash. Many treaties were signed by the Indians under duress. During negotiations with the Osage Tribe in 1808, George C. Sibley, in giving an account of the negotiations, said that the Osages were told, if they signed the Treaty, they would be "considered friends of the United States, and treated accordingly. Those who refuse to come forward and sign shall be considered enemies of the United States and treated accordingly." The squeeze was really on, when in 1808 the Choctaws, being indebted to certain mercantile characters "beyond what could be discharged by the ordinary proceeds of their huntings, and pressed for payment by these creditors, proposed at length to the United States to cede lands to the amount of their debts, and designated them in two different portions of the country. Negotiations took place for some time, and finally the Choctaws were induced to cede to the U.S. five million acres of their land, described by Jefferson as "no inconsiderable portion of the first quality."

Thomas Jefferson authorized a surveying party to inspect the land from the boundaries of the nation to the Pacific Ocean, when he sent Meriweather Lewis on that journey of explora-

95

tion which resulted in the "opening of the West," and the ultimate destruction of Indian life west of the Mississippi. Jefferson was fascinated by all aspects of Indian life.

He kept a listing of vocabularies of various Indian languages. He noted details of Indian dress and manners, customs and religions. He never ceased to be interested in Indian mores and customs, maintaining an intellectual magnifying glass under which the Indian was inspected from many aspects, but never from the position of being a complete human being with rights and liberties common to all men.

Jefferson displayed the same concern for the natives, when the United States needed their friendship, that Washington had shown when the evolving union of states needed friendly tribes on their fighting flanks. In his instructions to Meriweather Lewis, he ordered the exploration party to ". . . make yourself acquainted with the names of the nations and their numbers, the extent and limits of their possessions; their relations with other tribes or nations; allay all jealousies as to the objects of your journey; make them acquainted with the position, extent, character, peaceable and commercial dispositions of the U.S., of our wish to be neighborly, and of our dispositions to a commercial intercourse with them." The Lewis and Clark expedition had, as its main purpose, the expansion of American commercial interests. It laid the basis for America's final acquisition and conquest of all the area between the Atlantic and Pacific.

Two other Virginians held the office of Chief Executive in succeeding terms of office, James Madison, who served from 1809 to 1817, and James Monroe, from 1817 to 1825. During Madison's tenure the great Chief Tecumseh was killed by General Harrison's men during the War of 1812. The deed was done on Canadian soil. General Andrew Jackson became a figure of note in this war. Having secured the friendly aid of the Creeks and the Cherokees in the war, he did not hesitate to turn on his friends. In July, 1814, Jackson demanded and got twenty-three million acres of Creek land, constituting three-fifths of Alabama and one-fifth of Georgia. It is true that the Creeks had chosen war rather than submit to white encroachment and forced land cessions, under whatever disguise. But by this time, the southern tribes, including the Creeks, Cherokees, Chickasaws, Choctaws, and Seminoles, were becoming assimilated into American life. Intermarriage was relatively common, especially among the families of chiefs. Indian life took on the aspect of an American state; the Indian state was largely modeled after the United States, complete with both Houses of Congress, courts and judiciary.

During Monroe's administration, the insistent voice of the southern states and the onrushing settlers began to hasten the final destruction of Indian landholdings in the south. Too, the Indians, who had adopted white man's plantation methods in the south, also possessed slaves. But the slaves of the tribes had a somewhat different character than those of the whites. The blacks intermarried with the Indians, becoming accepted into the tribes. Certain areas of the south, such as those in Florida, were sanctuaries for escaping slaves, and slave hunters penetrated Seminole country time and again in a relentless search for them. Slaves came to the Seminoles for refuge, from the North and the South, established their own villages and became part of the Seminole nation. When Andrew Jackson arbitrarily annexed Florida to the United States in 1818, he bitterly denounced the Indians, saying, "Negro brigades were establishing themselves when and where they pleased, with Seminole help."

President James Monroe, in his first annual message to Congress, on December 2, 1817, said " . . . the earth was given to mankind to support the greatest number of which it is capable, and no tribe or people have a right to withhold from the wants of others more than is necessary for their own support and comfort . . . " This philosophy gave the moral fibre needed to the land-grabbers and proponents of forced removal. But Monroe, sickened at the sight of manifest injustice to the Cherokees, said in 1824, in another message to the Congress, "To remove them (the Cherokees) from their present territory by force with a view to their own security and happiness, would be revolting to humanity and utterly unjustifiable." The policy of forced removal originally suggested by President Jefferson, was officially put into effect nevertheless by Secretary of War John C. Calhoun, under authority of President James Monroe, and carried out with merciless success by President Andrew Jackson.

Under Andrew Jackson's administration, the framework of future Indian policy was established. The country is suffering, even today, the results of this superstructure. In all, five important federal statutes were enacted. The Act of May 28, 1830, provided for Indian removal. The Act of July 9, 1832, established the post of Commissioner of Indian Affairs. On June 30, 1834, the Indian Trade and Intercourse Act was passed. On the same date, an Act was passed establishing the Department of Indian Affairs (still under the jurisdiction of the Department of War.) The Act of January 9, 1837, regulated the disposition of proceeds of ceded Indian lands. The powers of the President were clearly spelled out in all five statutes.

Jackson's fame rested largely on his reputation as one of the most ruthless "Indian fighters" in American history. It was Jackson who led the operations of the American Army against the Seminoles. His administration was studded with the blackest deeds in America's Indian history: Indian removal by force; the death of thousands of Indians upon the trail to the west; frauds flagrantly perpetrated upon Indians by land sharks; his refusal to abide by the treaties or even the laws of the land or the decision of the Supreme Court. Indeed, he is to be remembered not alone for his misdeeds against the Indian people. Among other interesting innovations in governmental immorality, the infamous Spoils System was inaugurated by Jackson.

During Jackson's regime, the Choctaws were removed from Mississippi without further negotiations. Five tribes of the south were ordered to move forthwith, from North Carolina, South Carolina, Georgia, Florida, Alabama and Mississippi, to Oklahoma Territory. Existing treaties were totally disregarded. When, under the laws of the United States, the Cherokees appealed to the Supreme Court, the appeal resulted in a decision favorable to the Indians by Chief Justice Marshall, President Jackson is then said to have remarked, "John Marshall has made his decision; let him enforce it." Immediately following the passage of the Removal Act, hundreds of white squatters entered Creek territory. Squatters took the cornfields planted by the Sauks, and the Indians had to cross Rock River to steal their own corn in order to live. Several treaties were executed under Jackson's orders which later proved to be fraudulent, including the Treaty at Paynes Landing, in 1832, the interpreter deliberately falsifying the translation of the treaty with the Seminoles. In 1832, the treaty with the Chickasaws ceded outright all of its land to the United States. The alternative was forced removal by surrounding whites at the point of a gun; or forced removal by the government to any place decided upon by the Indian agents. These people were overrun by whites even before the agreed-upon removal took place

The war against the natives was not restricted to the southern tribes. In 1834, while trappers attempted to raid some Hopi gardens in the Southwest. The Hopis resisted. The trappers shot twenty Hopi People. In 1837, towards the end of the Jackson era of infamy, the United States acquired 26 million acres of Indian land, for three cents an acre. In that year, slavers invaded Indian camps in Florida, seizing Indian and black children, men and women indiscriminately. In October, the Seminoles came in to surrender and parley for peace, under a white flag. They were murdered, in violation of international convenants, their leader Osceola being taken at the same time.

During the Jackson era, seventy-four treaties were concluded with the tribes, all of them under duress and threat of having their lands taken whether or not the tribes signed. Finally, it is interesting to note President Jackson's understanding of the Presidential office, and how it should be run: "The Congress, the Executive and the Court must each for itself be guided by its own opinion of the Constitution. Each public officer who takes an oath to support the Constitution swears that he will support it as he understands it, and not as it is understood by others . . . the opinion of the judges has no more authority over Congress than the opinion of Congress has over the judges, and on that point the President is independent of both."

Jackson's policies were faithfully carried out by President Martin Van Buren, who took office in 1837. Regarding Cherokee removal, President Van Buren said in December, 1838, with incredible cynicism, " . . . the measures authorized by Congress at its last session have had the happiest effects. The Cherokees have migrated without any apparent reluctance." Let it be noted that the Cherokee homeland constituted approximately forty thousand square miles in the Valley of the Tennessee, protected by treaties, agreements, and mutual covenants of friendship between the United States and the Cherokee Nation. After removal, some tribes received lands upon which others had already settled. Nevertheless, there were leaders who desired some form of unity for purposes of sheer survival. Such efforts were discouraged, in a report of Commissioner of Indian Affairs T. Hartley Crawford in 1838, who said, " . . . prudential considerations would seem to require that they should be kept distinct from each other . . . ''

In 1849, with the administration of President Zachary Taylor, the Department of the Interior was established, and the Secretary of the Interior, under Title 5, Section 485 of the United States Code, now had supervision over public business relating to the Indians, and by Title 25, Section 2 of the Code, the Commissioner of Indian Affairs was given supervision over the management of Indian affairs under the direction of the Interior Secretary, "according to regulations prescribed by the President."

During the years 1846 through 1852, a new era of Indian exploitation was opened. The United States, in its war with Mexico, acquired the California and other western territories. On May 12, 1848, the existence of gold in quantity in California was made public by Samuel Brannan, a bishop of the Mormon Church. From then on, the process of destruction of Indian lands, Indian lives, and Indian cultures reached a high point in American history. By the Treaty of Guadalupe Hidalgo with Mexico, the Indians were assured of protection, and of the right to citizenship. These rights were ignored. Instead, a system of genocide became the rule, especially in the gold mining country. In 1851, the United States sent three commissioners to negotiate treaties with the Indian tribes of California, and 18 such treaties were signed with the reluctant Indians, who were forced to give up the whole of California for the right to survive in small regions of the state. The Senate refused to ratify the California treaties, as the result of an outcry by the California legislature, which insisted upon taking the land from the tribes.

The Indians of the California tribes kept their part of the treaty bargain. The United States Government did not. Neither were the Indian tribes informed of the United States Senate's failure to ratify the treaties, so that they might demand the return of their land.

Under President Millard Fillmore, from 1850 to 1858, the following lands were taken from the Indian tribes either by forced treaty, under duress at the point of a gun, or through organized and deliberate armed conflict. The Willamette Valley Tribes gave up 7,500,000 acres for $198,000. The Walla Walla, Cayuse and Umatilla Tribes yielded 4,012,800 acres, for $150,-000. The Yakima, Pelouse, Klickitat, and other bands in the state of Washington gave the United States 10,828,000 acres for which $200,000 was paid. The Des Chutes surrendered 8,110,000 acres for $135,000. The Flathead, Kootenai, Upper Pend D'Oreilles, were forced to deliver 14,720,000 acres for $485,000, and the Rogue River Indians on September 10, 1853, had wrested from them 2,180,000 acres, for which they received a paltry $60,000, or three cents an acre, giving the tribe approximately $2.75 each as annual income. Under this condition, the tribe was reduced from nearly 2,000 in 1853, to 909 in 1858.

In more recent times, through the Court of Claims and the federal Indian Claims Commission, many tribes have received additional sums of money, after costly and long litigation. But no amount of money was ever compensated the Indian tribes for their destroyed economy and culture, resulting from the taking of their land and means of livelihood. The entire continent was either taken forcibly or given up under false pretenses, by the Indian tribes, in payment for which the United States Government promised to deliver certain services, funds, and rights to such economic necessities as hunting and fishing. From time to time there occurs an outcry from certain people in the dominant society, demanding to know why the Indians are receiving certain services, are tax free on their reservations, and demand the right to hunt and fish on their aboriginal native land and waters. It is seldom known, and often forgotten that the promised services and funds were not delivered, even though some small beginnings have been made today in such areas as education—and then only after constant struggle on the part of the Indian people. It is certainly not accepted by most representatives of the United States Government, and by some of the general public, that the Indians ceded their land and that these services and funds are *in payment for land surrendered.*

Without detracting from the reputation of America's Abraham Lincoln, he of the lowly beginnings, it must be stated as a matter of historic truth that President Lincoln's administration was marked with wars against the natives. The Apaches fought for three years for their independence, their land and their homes, against steadily encroaching squatters, settlers, and frontiersmen. In the time of Lincoln, drought struck the Hopi villages in Arizona Territory. A Hopi delegation pleads for aid and is thrown into jail. The Territory had no help for the starving Hopi. In 1863, the Territory of Arizona was created, and the state legislature forthwith called for extermination of the Apaches. In 1863, gold was found in Prescott, Arizona. At Bloody Tanks (modern Miami in Arizona), white settlers under the guise of a peace conference poisoned twenty-four Apaches. This incident in known as the Pinole Treaty in the Tonto Basin. The Apaches were enraged again when Lincoln's General Carleton established Fort Bowie inside Apache territory without Indian consent. The general's avowed policy was extermination. In 1862, there were Sioux uprisings in Minnesota, and the battle of Yellow Medicine took place, in which new armaments were brought to bear successfully against the Indians. In 1863 the Nez Perce Indians were forced to leave their home in Wallowa Valley, in eastern Oregon, for an Idaho reservation. The removal of the Concow Indians from Chico, California, took place in 1863, another "Trail of Tears" in which hundreds of these Maidu people died enroute to Round Valley, their place of captivity.

In 1863, J. Harlan, agent for the Cherokee Indians from Tahlequah Agency in Oklahoma Territory, reported that, "Twenty-five years after removal from their homeland . . . their destitution is almost complete . . . There are no schools in the Nation. From being once proud, intelligent and wealthy . . the Cherokee are now stripped of nearly all . . . The Cherokee Indians have not received the protection stipulated in the treaty with them . . . They have no clothing or blankets for the winter, and food for but sixty days." Many Cherokees joined the Confederate Army, having developed an overwhelming hatred for the northern whites, who from Washington on down in the bureaucracy, refused to keep the treaty made by them, which the Indians had kept in good faith.

On November 29, 1864, the Cheyenne and Arapahoe came to make peace in Kansas and Colorado Territory. They were ordered to occupy a campsite on Sand Creek. The peaceful village was then attacked by troops commanded by Col. John M. Chivington. The name of the Sand Creek Massacre has now achieved a place in the history as one of the bloody dates of the Lincoln administration. Again in 1864, Col. Kit Carson herded 8,000 Navajos to Bosque Redondo, where they remained in captivity until 1868.

During the administration of President Andrew Johnson, 1865 to 1869, a new element is introduced in the affairs of the government with Indian tribes. Various tribes are "assigned" to different churches for missionary work, with military impartiality, "to give each denomination a fair show at the heathens." In general, the policy of annexation, cession, expropriation, and plundering of Indian land continued. On November 23, 1868, General George Custer attacked a peaceful encampment of Cheyenne, Kiowa, Arapahoe and Apache people, and Black Kettle, Cheyenne leader, was killed.

Under President Grant's administration, certain facts of fraud by some officials in the Indian service were uncovered. Much later, in 1911, Commissioner Robert G. Valentine was to report, "Indian affairs are, even under the best possible administration, peculiarly a field for the grafter, and all other wrongdoers. The lands and the moneys of the Indian offer a bait which the most satiated fish will not refuse." Disclosures of wrongdoing in the Grant administration led to the creation of a Board of Indian Commissioners in 1929, the Board members to be appointed by the President, to whom they were to report. The Board was abloished, after exposing some of the most horrifying details of mismanagement in Indian affairs, in 1933.

With the end of treaty-making in 1871, the conquest of the Indian race on the North American continent was a recognized fact. The action was taken through the passage of the Appropriations Act of 1872, approved March 3, 1871 (16 Stat. L. 566) which had this clause tacked on to the section on appropriations for the Yankton Indians, "Hereafter, no Indian nation or tribe within the territory of the United States shall be acknowledged or recognized as an independent nation, tribe, or power with which the United States may contract by treaty." However, provision was made for continuation of the conditions of all prior treaties. In the light of later assertions by ignorant politicians and misinformed historians, that the treaties made with the Indians were of no effect, "merely face saving devices," as one historian states, the fact that it was considered necessary to place into congressional legislation an *end* to treaty making with the Indians, and to assert the rights of the former treaties, makes one wonder whether indeed reason has not fled from the minds of such people.

Presidential or Congressional Agreements continued, however, to be made with the tribes, sometimes consummated by Executive Order, and sometimes by congressional legislation. The agreements had the same force, actually, as the treaties. Grant's regime is further distinguished by the discovery of gold

103

in the Black Hills of the Sioux country, which induced a government "reconnaissance" to explore the country, under General George A. Custer. This action was described as a "military necessity" at the time, but the presence of miners and prospectors in Custer's group, who excavated, reported, explored, and took samples of the precious metal, exposed it as a thinly disguised mercenary expedition. Finally, in 1876, the Black Hills contained nearly a thousand encroaching miners. The situation became tense when the Teton tribes, the Northern Cheyennes, Arapahoes and Yanktons objected to this violation of their lands, their treaties and their rights.

The administration of Ulysses S. Grant was crowned with an historic event, the battle of the Little Big Horn, in which the Sioux defeated the Custer forces on June 25, 1876. In the same year, the Nez Perce were subdued, and exiled to Fort Lincoln, then to Fort Leavenworth, then to the Quapaw Agency, then to the Salt Fork of the Arkansas River in 1879. In June, 1877, Chief Joseph of the Nez Perces began the long march to safety in Canada, fleeing from the marauding American forces. Only thirty miles from the border and safety, on October 3, 1877, Joseph was forced to surrender.

Of this period in the history of the American Indian, it was said in 1872 by Commissioner of Indian Affairs Francis A. Walker:

"Had the settlements of the United States not been extended beyond the frontier of 1867, all the Indians of the settlement would to the end of time have found upon the plains an inexhaustible supply of food and clothing. Were the westward course of population to be stayed at the barriers of today, notwithstanding the tremendous inroads made upon their hunting grounds since 1867, the Indians would still have hope of life. But another such five years will see the Indians of Dakota and Montana as poor as the Indians of Nevada and Southern California; that is, reduced to the habitual condition of suffering from want of food . . . The freedom of expansion which is working these results is to us of incalculable value. To the Indian it is of incalculable cost. Every year's advance of our frontier taken in a territory is as large as some of the kingdoms of Europe. We are richer by hundreds of millions, the Indian is poorer by a large part of the little that he has. This growth is bringing imperial greatness to the nation; to the Indian, it brings wretchedness, destitution, beggary."

President Chester A. Archur, 1881-1885, authorized the
Secretary of the Interior to give official approval to rules prohibiting "rites and customs . . . contrary to civilization." The
sacred and social dances, religious rites, and traditional rituals
were forbidden. This unconscionable abolition of the freedom to
worship, as established by the Bill of Rights, was defended by
the Commissioner of Indian Affairs in a report for 1885: "There
is no special law authorizing the establishment of such a court
(Court of Criminal Offenses), but authority is exercised under
the general provisions of law giving his Department supervision
of the Indians. The policy of the Government for many years
past has been to destroy the tribal relations as fast as possible." It would be fruitless to enumerate the continuing efforts
of the westward-marching nation to bring the natives under
complete subjection, or failing that, to "keep them quiet" in
the isolation of reservations known in more modern times as
concentration camps. The Indians in many cases rebelled, but
unsuccessfully. Yet the story of their stubborn resistance is
epic. Some descendant of the people will one day write this epic.

The next most important political event in the history of
the American Indian was the enactment of the Dawes Act,
better known as the General Allotment Act, which was passed
on Feburary 8, 1887 (24 State. L. 338). The Act authorized the
President to make allotments whenever in his opinion any reservation should be suitable for agricultural or grazing purposes.
Various amendments to the Dawes Act continued to be made
until 1933, when it ended. Under the amendment of June 25,
1910, the President was given authority to determine the size
of allotments, with a maximum limit of thirty acres of agricultural land and one hundred and sixty acres of grazing land.
Despite its much advertised advantages in "civilizing" the Indian, conditions grew immensely worse during the course of the
Act.

Actually, as one report stated, the Allotment Act was just
another attempt to "scrap the treaties without paying damages
in hard cash." The land allotment system broke up the tribal
domain into individual holdings. Such small parcels of land could
be rented to whites and sold to whites upon the death of the
allottee. In the course of this Act, Indian lands were cut down
from 139 million acres in 1887, to 47 million acres in 1930. A
uniform pattern of general law and regulations was sought.
But the political autonomy of the tribes, and the people them-

selves, were totally ignored. A survey, authorized by the Senate in 1928, finally brought to light the abuses and failures of the Allotment Act.

"Allotment" did not end without inflicting some of the worst wrongs upon Indian culture and life. Such wrongs were wrought out of the complete lack of understanding on the part of the leaders and particularly on the part of the nation's Chief Executives. For example, President Theodore Roosevelt lauded the Dawes Act in these words, ". . . The General Allotment Act is a mighty pulverizing engine to break up the tribal mass . . . We should now break up the tribal funds . . . we should definitely make up our minds to recognize the Indian as an individual and not as a member of a tribe . . . In the schools the education should be elementary and largely industrial. The need of higher education among the Indians is very, very limited."

One of the most important events in the administration of Theordore Roosevelt was the decision of the Supreme Court in the case of Lone Wolf vs. Hitchcock, in which the Court held that Congress had plenary authority over tribal relations and that it might pass laws to abrogate the provisions of a treaty. The war of extermination against the native peoples was now more than three hundred years old.

Another side of the Indian story was told in the rapidly increasing toll of new diseases brought by Europeans. The Report of the Indian Commissioner in 1910 states, "On the Lapwai Reservation in Idaho . . . there is scarcely a family in a population of over 1,400 which has not one or more members affected by chronic or acute disease." In the southwest at some places, from 65 to 95 percent of the Indians were infected with trachoma. So indifferent to the plight of the Indian people were the dominant whites, that after Geronimo, the Apache Indian leader, was placed under the jurisdiction of the War Department at Fort Sill, he and his people were completely forgotten. In 1910, during President Taft's administration, the descendants of the original prisoners were still being kept at Fort Sill under War Department jurisdiction! During Taft's administration, frauds soon began to crowd the desk of the Indian Office in connection with obtaining allotments.

Allotments in connection with Indians of New York State involved forgery on the part of whites, illegal sales, and other fraudulent activities.

President Woodrow Wilson was too busy with World War I to pay any attention to the Indian problem, which did not go away with tho onset or the end of the war. However, during the course of the war, the tribes sent their young men voluntarily into the armed services, and at the end of the war, citizenship was made available to Indian participants in the services.

President Harding's administration saw the introduction of a comprehensive system of stealing from the United States government, primarily through the Secretary of the Interior, Albert B. Fall. His policy was the immediate and complete "exploitation of natural resources by private interests." He also declared that the Indian title to lands reserved to them by Executive Order was no title at all, and that these lands could be taken from them without compensation. At this time, in 1922, more than half the Indian land had been established by Executive Order. Fall also sponsored the Bursun Bill, which would have taken land and water from the Pueblos, and would have transferred Pueblo titles to whites. Secretary Fall promoted the so-called Indian Omnibus Bill, which passed the House of Representatives in 1923. This was another attempt to pulverize Indian life and take Indian land. It was finally defeated by a wave of Indian resentment and the actions of various Indian organizations in opposition to the bill. Harding's Secretary of the Interior was ultimately sent to prison for his misconduct and illegal, fraudulent activities in these and other matters.

In 1924, citizenship was granted to the American Indian, by Congressional action. The last of America's peoples thus attained the status of citizens. Even then, the states of Arizona and New Mexico did not grant this privilege until 1946 and 1948. The whole matter of Indian citizenship is filled with the same confusion of policy and contradiction in action as all other matters concerning Indian affairs. When the rights of citizenship were granted in 1924, certain individual rights were at the mercy of Congress. The right of the Indian, as a member of a certain tribe, is often in conflict with the rights and privileges of citizenship as an individual in the United States social and political system. Until 1885, the Bureau of Indian Affairs had authority to issue tribal "citizenship papers" to individuals claiming this privilege in the Eastern Band of Cherokees. Thus, many who were not Cherokees, not even Indians, were forced upon the Cherokees as tribal members authorized to share in funds, lands, and assets of the tribe. The Cherokees had to take this issue to court, the Supreme Court finally deciding that the Nation had sole power to determine all claims based on blood or descent to citizenship, in that nation. The record shows, however, that the Afro-American acquired citizenship in 1868, through Constitutional Amendment. Women obtained citizenship in 1920, in the same way. It seems a sad commentary that the native people of the land should have had to acquire their franchise in so many devious ways, through so much effort and so many setbacks, and finally through the back door of this country's governmental authority, by a Congressional action which may be altered once again at the pleasure of the same Congress.

The first attempt at "humanization" of the Indian Service came with the administration of Herbert Hoover in 1929. President Hoover named the distinguished Ray Lyman Wilbur, president of Stanford University, as Secretary of the Interior, and Charles J. Rhoades, his Commissioner of Indian Affairs. Elected with Hoover as vice president was Charles Curtis, son of a Kaw woman and the first Indian to be elected to high government office. Hoover and his Interior staff were able to affect some changes in the school system of the Bureau of Indian Affairs, such as the attempt to stop corporal punishment, and the enforced taking of Indian children from their homes without parental consent.

In 1930, a Senate Investigating Committee exposed conditions revealing the systematic kidnapping of Indian children from Navajo parents on the reservation. Despite the efforts and the investigation, however, conditions continued to worsen.

President Hoover's broad humanitarianism was not supported by an understanding of the Indian people, their history or culture. His policy was to "fuse them with the general population" as quickly as possible." He believed that only in this way would the Indian fall heir to American individualism, which to Hoover was the highest privilege of any human being. He failed to see the possibility and even the urgent need of a quite different culture existing side by side with America's European culture.

In 1933, the "Indian New Deal" was born under the Roosevelt administration. Thereupon, from 1933 to 1945, the "Indian Problem" became a matter of intense public debate. Roosevelt chose, as Commissioner of Indian Affairs, a well-known propagandist, John Collier. From this administration came the Wheeler-Howard Act, known also as the Indian Reorganization Act. The IRA was lauded for "organizing" Indian society. It was forgotten that long before European settlement upon this continent, the Iroquois Confederacy was established, which drafted a constitution soon to be the model for the Constitution of the United States. The Act finally resulted in imposition of conditions upon the tribes which were alien to their best interests, and established the Secretary of the Interior as the sole determining agent over tribal affairs, a final authority without possibility of appeal, who could accept or reject any action of any tribe, and could even void the constitution of a tribe without authorization, consent, or consultation with the people.

By this time, it had become evident that no matter what legislation was enacted, or what humane forces were at work operating in favor of the tribes, the governmental policy of administering Indian affairs entirely through Title 25 of the U.S. Code (Indians) would continue. Even today, such questions as transfers of allotments, leasing of lands, disposition of funds, contracting for industry on reservation lands, leasing such assets as lumbering, oil and metal producing lands, must be approved by the Secretary of the Interior. Heirship matters must have the approval of the Secretary. Tribal actions, ordinances, and expenditures of funds must be approved by the Interior Secretary, as well as changes in constitutions of the tribes—all must be authorized and approved by the Secretary of the Interior. In quite recent times (1974) there is but one case that has come to attention, in which the tribe has presumably acted to consummate agreements involving leasing and there is not enough evidence to support this claim. This tribal action involved the Navajo Indian Nation.

Under the Collier Commissionership, attention was focused upon the plight of the Indians as never before. Indian religious practices received protection that had not been available hitherto. During this time, the Indian Arts and Crafts Board was established, resulting in a tremendous encouragement to the development of Indian art, and help to the Indian artist. Collier's regime saw many voluminous reports and studies. His administration was also noted for its infamous stock reduction program among the Navajo people, which reduced the tribe to poverty and provided no solution for the problem of over-grazing their land.

Collier and his colleagues, most of whom were anthropologists, spent seven years in exhaustive research, from 1940 to 1947. From all these researches there emerged one great "disconcerting finding . . . The Indian Service was falling far short of its opportunities . . . the falling-short were identified. They had their abode inside the institutional structure of the Government's Indian Service," said Collier. Finally, Commissioner Colliet noted with some dismay, that "There survived from the researches only a number of books of permanent importance." Soon, however, even before the end of the Roosevelt administration, dissatisfaction and dissension appeared.

The tribal councils, elected under the IRA, were charged with being "rubber stamps" for the Bureau of Indian Affairs. Dishonesty in elections was charged. Dishonesty in the handling of tribal funds was another accusation. Old-time Indian leaders saw the vestiges of Indian culture and life being destroyed or adulterated piecemeal. The last straw finally came, as Collier relates in his book, "From Every Zenith," when President Roosevelt vetoed a bill which had passed both Houses of Congress, in which the claim of the California Indians would have been settled for not less than $100,000,000. In Collier's words, his interview with the President went this way, "The President asked: Is there not some better way to do justice than by paying money damages? The Government's duty . . . is a duty to the future, not the past . . ."

The result of the Roosevelt veto was the continuation of litigation by the California tribes for another thirty-five years. The denial to them of historic justice, the continued refusal to them of services which were available to other citizens of the nation and a final "compromise settlement" to them of payment of forty-seven cents an acre for nearly all the land of California, which was taken from them in the 1850's, expressed one of the most outrageously unjust actions of the Roosevelt administration towards the Indian people.

The rest of the story relating to the role of the Presidents of the United States in the history of the American Indian is only a continuation of the weary, dreary miscarriage of historic justice towards the native peoples.

The Eisenhower administration vetoed a bill making payment to the Crow Indian Tribes, on June 8, 1956, on account of a right of way for a dam and reservoir. It was President Eisenhower who signed H.R. 1063, which became Public Law

280. This Act confers jurisdiction in certain states with respect to criminal offenses and civil causes of action committed or arising on Indian reservations in those states. In signing the bill, the President himself stated, ". . . I have grave doubts as to the wisdom of certain provision contained in H.R. 1063 . . ." The bill, in fact, has reduced still further Indian control over its economy, its society, and its culture, as well as its tribal laws. It has opened up a whole new possibility of civil actions which could result in acquisition of Indian land by whites, and criminal actions which could have the effect of punitive acts against the tribes.

President John Kennedy's administration was marred by his failure to veto the measure providing for the taking of Seneca lands in order to construct the Kinzua Dam in New York State. Kennedy might have invoked the Seneca Treaty and stopped the building of the dam. He could have simply vetoed the bill without any explanation other than the facts in the case—which were that the taking of the Seneca land was unjust, illegal, and an outrage upon public decency.

Kennedy's grasp of Indian history and culture, in words, seemed so much more profound that his actions in practice as exemplified in the Kinzua Dam affair, that it only serves to bear out the assumption in this article, that there has always been and still continues to be, a broad and unbridgeable chasm between the heart and the hand in the administrative affairs of the Indian.

At least three presidential administrations were deeply involved in the approval for the rape of the Navajo reservation, also known as the Black Mesa strip mining project, which is pouring filth and destruction upon both the Hopi and the Navajo reservations, corrupting the land, and destroying Indian economy. Presidents Eisenhower, Kennedy, and Johnson were all involved in this project. It was that "great and humane supporter of Indian economic improvement" Interior Secretary Stewart Udall, who finally consummated the contract which the Navajos and Hopis both will find an unbearable burden in terms of destruction of life and land.

The administration of President Lyndon Johnson is marked by the same historical bureaucracy, the same unconstitutional usurpation of Indian leadership and independence, and the same errors which have been made down through the centuries in the affairs of the Indian people. It is true that more money is being spent today than ever before, and for more purposes. At the same time, the money is being spent for more officials, more bureaucrats, more administration, than at any time in our history. And the old song is still being sung.

For example, in the Act of October 14, 1966, it is stated that, "... funds ... shall be divided on the basis of tribal membership rolls, after approval of such rolls by the Secretary of the Interior." Under Section 2 of another Act, it is stated, "The Secretary of the Interior shall prepare membership rolls for the Quileute and Hoh Tribes." Under Public Law 89-660, as to the disposition of the funds of the Duwamish Tribe in Oregon, it is stipulated, "The determination of the Secretary of the Interior regarding the utilization of available rolls or records and the eligibility for enrollment of an applicant shall be final."

Those words, "authorized by the tribal government and approved by the Secretary of the Interior," may be the new rhythm of the song, but the tune is the same. Every Act of Congress and every regulation issued by authority of the President and the Department of the Interior bears these words, "as authorized by the Secretary of the Interior." There is really no difference, if the "tribal councils" are also concerned in decision making, if their decisions may not be final, but must be subjected to the scrutiny and review, and the final approval of a governmental officer.

The current administration of President Richard M. Nixon is famous for his assertion of support for Indian sovereignty, his exposure of the conflict of interests existing in the United States Governmental handling of Indian affairs, all of which were expressed in his famous message of 1970. The Indian tribes dare to hope. The money is flowing into tribal economy. Education is being made available to Indian youth on the highest level, and Indian-directed schools are being created. Indeed, the hopes of many tribes are so high, that a recent article in *Wassaja*, the national Indian newspaper, pointing to an excess of funds for administration of the funded programs, brought cries of anguish from several tribal leaders, which support the paper, approve its objective policy, and attest to its growing influence among the Indian people, that such criticism might impair their funding, and cause dissatisfaction among the tribesmen.

Nevertheless, we do not forget that it was President Nixon who vetoed the Indian Education Act, which was then taken to the courts through intensive Indian protest, there to have the Presidential impoundment lifted. We do not forget that the fifty-year old erosion of Indian water rights is worse now than it has ever been, and that non-Indians, as well as the states, are diverting Indian water, stealing Indian resources with the aid and approval of the Interior Department. It would appear that vigilance still continues to be the best posture for the Indian to adopt.

A recent bill introduced by the administration and passed by the Congress as part of the Nixon administration's "package of Indian legislation" is supposed to speed up the payment of Indian claims. The whole process has been "streamlined" to such a degree that the Interior Secretary has more power under this new Act than ever before, and the words, "as approved by the Secretary of the Interior still stand as a symbol of the heavy hand of the government holding back Indian independence, Indian self-determination, and Indian freedom to develop its economy and preserve its culture. In those words, and in such actions, resides the heart of the failure of the United States Government, from President George Washington to President Richard Nixon. Every action of the government, from now on, can be measured by these conditions, and every presidential candidate should be queried as to how and what he intends to do to change the government's basic failure to allow the Indian to lead his own people and to guide his own life.

A new way of life is opening up for all Americans. The shortage of oil, the shortage of energy, and the massive inflation in the economy which is stealing every advance made by the American citizen, both Indian and others, is bringing new disturbances to the American Indian. There is currently a monstrous pushing and shoving to lay hands on America's "last frontier," the lands and resources of the Native American. It is suddenly discovered that the Northern Cheyenne have coal on their land, the Navajos have minerals, the Montana and Wyoming tribes have minerals and coal, and the Alaska Natives have oil. Pressed on all sides by the needs of the general economy, the demands of the general populace, and the greed of the industrial magnates, can the American Indian hold out against this last "American expansion into a new frontier," a frontier which embraces the remnants of Indian lands and resources?

Note: At least seventy sources were consulted in connection with this article, and the space requirements make it impractical to list them all. Should such references be desired, please write to the publisher for a copy.

Part VII

A Chronology
of American Indian History

THE ORAL HISTORY of the Native American before European conquest is all but gone, buried in the memories of those who lived in this continent for more than 40,000 years. What we have now is evidence of landings on the North American continent, long before the voyage of the Italian Christopher Columbus. After that first invasion in 1492, Indian history is a continuous struggle against invasion, fraud, a period of treaty-making, and ultimate disaster.

From approximately 1100 to 1400, Norwegians landed on Iceland, traveled to the eastern seaboard of the North American continent, are known to have touched the shores of Alaska, and are said to have even landed on the shores of Florida. Norsemen were known as occasional visitors and took their place in native legendry. Legends also deal with the people of the north, as friends or enemies, as the case might be.

The landing of Christopher Columbus on the island in the Carribean known today as Haiti is not the most important evidence of European entry into North America.

Of far greater importance is the year 1494, when Columbus sent five hundred Indians to Spain to be sold into slavery. The Four Hundred Years' War had begun.

Thus, to put the history of the American Indian in proper perspective, contact with the Europeans should be dealt with in such a way as to indicate that:

The Indians of North America, in an island now known as Haiti, met a party of white men, whom they later grew to know as the Christopher Columbus invaders. In a matter of a few years, most of the Indians on that island had been wiped out. In 1494, the Indians were sold into slavery in Spain.

1501. In Labrador, fifty-seven Indians are captured to be sold as slaves in Europe. The Portuguese had attacked the Indians, but on the way home, the ship sank with all aboard.

1511. Hathvey, Indian chief of Cuba, is captured. Under the leadership of the Spanish priest, Las Casas, he is burned alive. A priest, exhorting him to acknowledge Christ and the Christian faith, saying that he could then go to heaven, receives this reply from Hathvey: "Let me go to hell that I may not come where you are."

1519-1520. The invasion of Mexico begins, with Cortez leading an army having highly superior arms. Soon the land is occupied by the Spanish, the Aztec leader Montezuma is killed, and a long war begins between the Indian people and the Spanish.

1526. Indians on the Carolina coast defend themselves against the Spanish settlers under Vasquez de Ayllon, who brings five hundred men, women and children to remove the Indians from their land. The Indians are victorious and the settlement disappears.

1528. The Karankawa Indians of Texas feed and care for the survivors of a Spanish shipwreck, who were practicing cannibalism in a vain effort to remain alive. The survivors are welcomed as guests by the Karankawa people, who are later repaid for their pains by having their land taken from them by the invaders.

1532. Thousands of unarmed Inca Indians are slaughtered by Pizarro in Peru. The priest-chief, Atahualpa is held for ransom. He is ransomed for $30,000 in gold. Atahualpa is then strangled to death by the Pizarro soldiers.

1534. The Mayos and Yaqui Indians begin to resist Spanish aggression.

1539. The Zuni Indians resist the Spaniards of Coronado's expedition, killing Estevan who was serving with the expedition. Pueblo resistance against foreign invasion begins.

1540. The Zuni villagers are again attacked by Coronado, and the villages are destroyed. When a Hopi village resists the invaders, it is destroyed.

1541. Religion of the Indians in northern Mexico is forbidden by the Spanish. Acoma Pueblo is attacked by Coronado. The Tigua resist Spanish domination and enslavement. Two hundred men are burned at the stake. The Choctaws refuse demands from De Soto to provide bearers for his invading forces. They succeed in driving the invaders from their land, killing De Soto.

1565. An Indian village, just outside St. Augustine, is attacked by Spaniards, and all are slaughtered.

1568. Indian children are kidnapped and taken to Havana, Cuba. There the Jesuit priests organize a school for them, attempting to indoctrinate them in the Christian religion.

1570 (1490?). Two dates are given for the founding of the League of the Six Nations. Their system of democratic government is the most liberal in the world at this time. This group first included the Mohawk, Oneida, Seneca, Cayuga and Onondaga. The Tuscarora were admitted later, under patronage of the Oneida.

1584. Indians living off the coast of North Carolina meet a party of English colonists who land on Roanoke Island. During the years 1585-86, the colonists either blend with the Indian population, or are lost. There is no further word about them.

1585. Several Indian villages are burned to the ground in Sir Richard Grenville's Virginia settlement. Men, women and children are killed. Many are sold into slavery.

1587. Indians living off the coast of North Carolina meet still another party of colonizers under their Governor John White. White leaves the colonists to sail home. When he returns three years later, they are not to be seen. This group of colonists becomes known as the "Lost Colony," and only the Indians know what has become of them. The natives have blended with the newcomers, and have begun a new element in Indian society.

1589. The Pueblo Indians are shocked to see a contingent of four hundred Spanish men, women and children, with more than eighty wagons and seven thousand head of cattle. They have come to settle in the Pueblo land, without permission of the natives.

1591. The Pecos River Tribes resist slave raids by the

117

Spaniards. They are conquered by two hundred soldiers under Castana de Sosa, and their resistance is crushed.

1599. Acoma Pueblo is taken by the Spanish after a bloody battle with Onate. The village is destroyed and eight hundred Indians are killed, five hundred and eighty are captured, most of whom are women. They are sentenced to slavery for twenty years. Each of the men is sentenced to having a hand or a foot cut off.

The Jivarros in Peru launch a revolt against their Spanish invaders, which at this time is successful.

1607. The Powhattan Indians learn that the Europeans plan to found their own colony, and they oppose the plan.

The Yaquis in Mexico defend themselves against an attack by Hurdaide. They defeat the Spanish. Captain Hurdaide returns and is again defeated by the Yaquis.

1609. Indian sovereignty takes on international significance when the English Crown reaffirms by law the "sovereignty of Indian nations."

A Mohawk longhouse is invaded by Champlain, who attacks the Indians with muskets. Many Mohawks are killed.

1615. An Oneida village is attacked by Champlain. The Indians drive him off.

1616. The Tarahumaras rise up against the Spanish. Hundreds of the Spanish are killed. It took two years to put down the rebellion. At the end, more than one thousand Indians had been killed.

1619. The Indians sign a treaty of trade and friendship with two Dutch traders at Tawagonshi in New York. This is believed to have been the first treaty between Europeans and the Indians.

1621. A Massachusetts chief, Obbatinua, signs a treaty with Miles Standish at Plymouth. This treaty has been questioned, since the date of the treaty (September 13, 1621) is eight days before the two men met.

1622. The Powhattan Confederacy attacks the Jamestown settlements, destroying the plantations and killing the invaders. They are led by Opechancanough, a Susquehannock chief.

1623. The tribes of Massachusetts plan an uprising against the English. Massasoit the traitor informs Miles Standish of the plan. Standish declares war on the tribes of Massachusetts. The Indians had objected to the taking of their land by the English, the destruction of their crops, and the forced labor exacted by the English.

1624. The Iroquois make a treaty with the French

1626. The Shinnecock Indians accept $24 from the Dutch
on May 6, and the Dutch believe they have purchased Manhattan Island. Purchase of land, however, was unknown by the
Indians, who believed they had merely permitted the foreigners
to use the land.

1629. The Pueblos see the establishment of missions, and
dissension begins to grow among the people. Some wish to
accept the missions; others do not. There are efforts to place
the Pueblos in feudal bondage, which are resisted.

1633. The Hopi continue to resist the invasion of the Cath-
olic faith upon their own religious beliefs and practices. The
Zuni kill the missionaries living among them.

A smallpox epidemic rages among the Pequot Indians. They were the tribesmen who had welcomed the Pilgrims.

1637. The eastern tribes are subjected to genocide by the
Dutch and English. Many Pequot are massacred. Some are sold
into slavery. In one village, two hundred are killed. Those
taken prisoner are placed in slavery, the slaves being divided
between Massachusetts and Connecticut. The rest are sent as
slaves to the West Indies. The Indians had resisted incursions
into their land and destruction of their economy by the Europeans.

1641. One half of the Mayos in Mexico are wiped out by
European epidemics.

The Raritan Nation, in an effort to regain their
land, attacks Staten Island, New York.

1642. The Shinnecock are massacred by Dutch settlers in
New York. The attack is headed by Dutch Governor Kieft
(who introduced scalping into North America) and Sergen Ru-
dolf with their soldiers. The date of this massacre, February
25, has gone down in the annals of history as the most brutal
in America. Unbelievable atrocities are committed by the killers.

1644. Indians of Massachusetts Bay Colony are forbidden to
come into town or into the houses of the English on Sunday,
unless it is to attend public meetings.

1648. The Tarahumara Indians rise in revolt against the
Spanish. They are defeated and their leaders are executed.

1649. Dissension among the tribes erupts in armed conflict
over support to the European invaders. The Iroquois put one
thousand men into the field, in battle against the Hurons, who

119

support the French. The battle takes place near the shore of Ontario's Georgian Bay. Many Hurons are killed, and two French Jesuit missionaries are dead.

1650. The Tarahumaras are again in revolt against the mission system of slavery, but the rebellion is put down.

1652. The Tarahumaras rebel again. Their rebellion is crushed once more, and their leader, Teporame, is executed.

1655. The Hopi are subjected to discipline by Father de Guerra, who punishes the Hopi Juan Cuna for "an act of idolatry." Cuna is beaten to unconsciousness, again beaten inside the church, and then doused with turpentine and set afire. The continuing struggle of the Hopi people to maintain their religion and culture again surfaces.

1656. The Yuchi Indians in Virginia defeat the English.

Indian reservations are planned by the United Colonies, meeting in Virginia. The native people are unaware of this plan, but their fate is sealed as plans are made to contain them in restricted areas in their own land.

1661. The Pequot War erupts in Rhode Island against the English and their allies, the Narragansetts and Mohegans.

Chief Massasoit of the Wampanoags dies. He had ceded nearly all of the tribe's land to the Europeans, without authorization from the tribe.

The Franciscan priests issue a decree prohibiting the Pueblos from practicing their religion. Kivas are raided, the masks are removed, and ceremonial equipment is destroyed.

Indians in Virginia are required to wear plaques when visiting British settlements. This is a predecessor to the Nazi requirement that Jews be identified in Germany.

1662. Smallpox wipes out thousands of Iroquois and Susquehannahs.

The Seri Indians in Mexico are attacked by Spaniards, and three hundred men, women and children are killed. Seri children are distributed among the Spanish after this defeat.

Alexander, the son of Massassoit, friend of the Pilgrims to the detriment of his own people, is arrested and subjected to interrogation by the British. Philip is also questioned and intimidated. The two brothers are humiliated in many ways.

1664. Several Canadian tribes sign a treaty of friendship with the English.

1670. The Zuni people rebel against religious oppression

by the missionaries.

1671. Philip is again subjected to interrogation by the British. They ask whether he is preparing an uprising.

1672. On October 7, White Mountain Apache raid Hawikum, largest of the Zuni Pueblos, in an attempt to rid the Pueblos of missionary control. They kill the friar, Pedro de Abila y Ayala.

1675. A group of young Wampanoag enter Swansea, Massachusetts, to protest the grazing of cattle on their land, which is destroying their crops. They shoot some cattle. The settlers abandon their homes for several days.

The Wampanoag, led by Philip, organize to rid themselves of white rule. On June 24, Philip leads an attack against the English in the southern part of New England. The war has begun in earnest. The Wampanoag attack and burn the settlements of Rehoboth, Taunton, Dartmouth, and Middleburrough. Fighting continues till August. Northfield and Deerfield are attacked in September. On September 28, Northampton is burned. On October 5, the Indians attempt to remove the whites from their land, and Springfield is burned. The English strike back in December, attacking the villages of the Narragansetts and burning to death six hundred non-combatants.

1676. War of the Wampanoag, joined by other tribes, continues under the leadership of Philip. These towns are attacked: Sudbury, Groton, Medfield, Lancaster, Marlborough, Andover, Woburn, Billerica, Chelmsford, Braintree, Weymouth, and Scituate (all in Massachusetts).

In Connecticut, Wickford, Warwick, Simsbury, Longmeadows and Northampton are attacked. In the Plymouth area, Bridgewater, Rehoboth, Providence and Plymouth itself are attacked. The tide of battle turns when traitors begin to appear. Bribery and promised pardons lead many to the capture of the leaders of the revolt. Canonehet is executed at Stonington. He had led the Narragansetts. Alderman, a traitor, offered to lead the English to the Wampanoag hideouts on August 6. On August 12, Philip (Metacomet), betrayed by Alderman, is put to death. On August 25, Quinapen is executed by the English in Newport, Rhode Island. He led the Swamp fight during the war of Philip. The War of the Wampanoags leaves the Indians defeated.

1680. This is the year of the Pueblo revolt against Spanish slavery and religious persecution. Pueblo land was reclaimed by the Indians, but the retreating Spanish carry off one hundred slaves which they sell into bondage in Mexico, forcing the Tigua Indians to act as bearers to El Paso. A battle takes place in the streets of Santa Fe, and the Spanish begin a mass exodus from Pueblo country. More than 2,500 Pueblo Indians engage in this battle, on August 21. A few Spanish survivors remain, but on October 21, they too abandon Santa Fe, leaving New Mexico to the Pueblo people.

1682. The Delaware Indians agree to treaty talks with William Penn.

1684. The Apaches in Mexico rebel. They are defeated and seventy-seven of their leaders are executed.

1686. The Delawares consummate a treaty with Penn.

1687. Iroquoian fishing parties are attacked and captured by the French on the St. Lawrence River.

1688. An army of twelve hundred Iroquois men invade the island of Montreal. They seek to revenge French cruelty to the Indians. More than a thousand French settlers are killed, the Iroquois losing three men.

1689. The Iroquois attack Lachine, Quebec, after the French had invaded their Longhouse. They remain two months, keeping the French penned up in their forts.

1690. The Tarahumaras rebel in Mexico against slave labor.

1692. The Pueblos are reconquered by the Spanish.

In the colony of Virginia, it is decided to banish all whites who marry Indians.

1694. The Tarahumaras are invaded by epidemics of measles and smallpox, brought by the invaders. Thousands die.

Jemez Pueblo rebels, supported by the Zuni. Both are defeated. Taos rebels, supported by the Pueblos of San Ildefonso, Santo Domingo, Acoma, Cochiti, and Picuris.

1696. The Pueblos are finally defeated, and are subject to Spanish law.

In Mexico, Apache are executed for resisting Spanish rule.

The Tarahumaras rebel. A general uprising ensues after Spanish atrocities are practiced, leading to outright war. The Indians refuse to surrender, choosing to die in battle. Thousands are killed.

1698. The Tarahumaras, choosing to go underground rather than to work as slaves of the Spanish and submit to Spanish rule, retreat into the inaccessible mountains.

1696. Onondaga and its stores of corn are destroyed by Frontenac. Oneida Castle is also destroyed by the French.

Thus ended the seventeenth century. This period began with the aggressive entry of Europeans into North America, who were greeted amicably by the Indians and received their aid, without which their survival was very questionable. Conflict soon arose when the Indians discovered the character of the invading force and their efforts to take their land. Dissension arose among the Indians themselves, when treacherous individuals chose to befriend the invaders, with no great benefit to the traitors. War erupted in full with the efforts of Philip (Metacomet) to drive the invaders from the land. This effort was defeated, in large part due to the treacherous actions of individual Indians, as well as to the superior arms of the British. The rebellion of the Pueblos took place in this century, with victory for the Pueblos at first, and defeat at the hands of the Spanish in consort with some Pueblos, in the end. The Tarahumaras rebelled again and again, finally being forced to flee to the mountains. Rebellion flared all over Indian country, wherever the whites entered the country, and the pattern was generally the same: friendly hospitality, repaid by slavery and intimidation, and final conquest by the invaders. The war was to continue, however, into the 19th century.

1700. The Ottawa tribe makes a treaty with the French in Montreal.

A treaty is proposed at Santa Fe, but is rejected by the Pueblo traditional leaders when the Spanish government refuses to restrict the activities of the missionaries. The Hopi destroy Awatovi and kill the Christianized Indians. They oppose the treaty. Governor Cubero moves to punish the Hopi, but he is not successful.

The Cherokee Indians now have the use of firearms.

1703. The Indians learn that bounties have been offered in Massachusetts for Indian scalps at the rate of $60 per scalp.

Apalachee Indians of Florida are attacked by white settlers and their Indian allies. Their towns are burned. More than two hundred are killed, and more than one thousand five hundred are sold into slavery.

The Five Nations Indians become British subjects, but they have no knowledge of this new international align-

123

ment, brought about through the Treaty of Utrecht, which ceded Arcadia, Newfoundland, and the Hudson Bay territory to England. Nor have they been consulted about their enforced allegiance to the British Crown.

1706. The Navajo people are subjected to repeated slave raids by the Spanish. The Navajo resist and are successful.

The Hopi defeat a Spanish force.

1712. The Yamasee Indians are raided for slaves. All the men of the tribe are killed. Women and children are taken for slaves.

The Tuscarora migrate from the southeast coast to New York State due to the wars resulting from slavery.

1715. The Yamasee organize a rebellion against the North English.

1722. The Tuscarora Indians are admitted to the Iroquois Confederacy, becoming the sixth nation in the League of the Iroquois.

The Abnaki are attacked by an English expeditionary force, located around the French mission at Norridgewock. The Indians are defeated.

1723. Indian students are at this time attending William and Mary College in considerable numbers. A building is erected for their use, the Brafferton.

1729. The Natchez Indians are attacked by the French. Hundreds are massacred. Prisoners from this slaughter are shipped as slaves to Santo Domingo.

1730. Seven Cherokee chiefs and headmen embark on an international mission of negotiations with the British Court at London. They enter into an alliance known as "The Articles of Agreement" with the Lords Commissioners. Negotiations had started at Nequassee (now known as Georgia).

1737. The Penn treaty with the Delawares is finally consummated. The treaty stipulates that there will be no forced removal of the Delawares.

1738. Cherokee Indians in Georgia receive a major gift of the Europeans, smallpox, brought by white slave traders to Charleston, South Carolina, thence to Georgia. Nearly half of the tribe is destroyed by the disease.

1740. This is the year of the Yaqui-Mayo rebellion. The Indians were protesting the taking of their land, and the enslavement of their people. They had sent two of their leaders to the Mexican capitol for negotiating purposes. They did not return. The people then rebelled. In a battle at Otamçahui (the Hill of Bones), the Spanish, under Lt. Vildosola, slaughter five thousand Indians

1746. The Huron leader, Orontony, moves against the French. The Huron villages are destroyed.

The Paiutes and Halchidhomas are raided for slaves to be sold in Mexico.

1748. The Seri Indians, who had developed farms and irrigation systems, protested the distribution of their land in Mexica. Their protests lead to mass roundups and to deportation of whole communities to Guatemala. Only the Seri women and children are sent away into slavery. The Seri men demand the return of their women and children. The Governor tells them it is too late. It was not even known where these people had been sent. A war follows.

1751. The Pima Indians organize a rebellion against the Spaniards and the missionaries in November. The Spanish governor responds by installing a special garrison of soldiers. The Pima leader is Oacpicagigua.

1758. The Lenape and Unami are placed on a reservation set up by the state of New Jersey. It is called Brotherton, and is comprised of one thousand six hundred acres of the Indians' own land.

1759. Alaskan natives are killed by members of the Russian expedition led by Pushkareff. There are raids into Alaska for slaves.

A Delaware prophet calls for a holy war against the whites, recommending that only traditional weapons be used.

1763. The War of the Ottawas begins, led by Pontiac. The Indians attack Detroit and several other English forts. They are successful. Germ warfare then begins against the Indians, when Lord Jeffrey Amherst, the British commander, distributes smallpox-infested blankets to the Indians. A widespread epidemic starts.

The Paxton boys destroy a settlement of Christian Indians at Lancaster, Pennsylvania.

1765-66. Two treaties are made between the Canadian Indians and the British Crown. These treaties recognize the equal sovereignty of the British Crown and the Iroquois, but also establish that the British have the right to make laws for the Indians. The treaties are known historically as the "Two Row Treaty," and the "Silver Calumet Treaty."

1768. The Six Nations are forced to surrender all the lands between the Ohio and the Tennessee rivers to the English. But the Iroquois had ceded land to which they had no right.

1769. Pontiac is assassinated.

The Indians of San Diego are thunderstruck to see the Spanish missionaries and soldiers. They see a wooden symbol, which they are told must be worshipped. It makes no sense to them, but they welcome the visitors, only to learn very shortly that they are now forced laborers and slaves.

1775. Becerro, the leader of the Seri, as he is dying, kills the Governor Mendoza, who was responsible for the kidnapping and deportation of Seri women and children to Guatemala.

A group of Cherokee Indians migrates to Arkansas.

1777. Chief Dragging Canoe and the Cherokees are forced to sign treaties ceding large tracts of their land.

1778. The Delaware sign a treaty with the newly-established United States Government. Statehood for the Delaware tribe is promised, with a seat in Congress. This was never accomplished, for unknown reasons. This treaty with the Delawares, on September 17, was the first treaty made by the United States with an Indian Nation.

1779. Many of the Iroquois continue to fight against the United States. During a campaign against the Indians, General John Sullivan destroys numerous brick and stone houses, hundreds of acres of vegetables and fruit, and many orchards. Trees are ringed.

1780. The Hopi and Zuni Indians are ravaged by smallpox.

1782. Christian Delawares are massacred at Gnanenhutten, Ohio. Previously, the English had advised them to move to Sandusky in order to avoid conflict with white settlers. But they sent back small groups to harvest their planted fields in the old place. These harvesters are found by a group of one hundred white men under Col. David Williamson. The Indians are killed with their own weapons. The Indians pray and sing hymns while thirty-five men, twenty-seven women, and thirty-four children are brutally slaughtered.

The Yuma Indians are in revolt, wiping out the missions, and destroying all vestiges of Spanish oppression.

A Huron Indian, L. V. Sabatannen, is the first Canadian-born individual to receive a college degree, at Dartmouth.

1785. The Cherokee, Catawba, Creek, Chickasaw, Choctaw and other tribes are forced to sign the Treaty of Hopewell, ceding millions of acres of land in Kentucky, Tennessee, North Carolina and other areas to the Americans.

A campaign of extermination is fully launched against the Apache. They have resisted for one hundred years, and the policy of the United States is now to exterminate them. Alcohol is introduced among them to demoralize them.

1789. Delaware Indians migrate in small groups to Missouri.

1790. Indians of the Northwest Ohio Territory are attacked by an expedition of four hundred armed men, known as the Miami Expedition, commanded by Col. John Hardin. They are ignominiously defeated, and the armed force retreats.

1791. Villages of the Wea Tribe are destroyed by United States troops.

The Seneca Indians write to General Washington, asking they be given teachers, so that "their men might be taught to farm and build houses, their women to spin and weave, and their children to read and write."

In October, 1791, Little Turtle attacks the forces of General Arthur St. Clair, governor of the Northwest Territory, and some one thousand four hundred militia on the Wabash River. St. Clair has casualties of nine hundred men.

1794. The Oneida, Tuscarora and Stockbridge Tribes sign a treaty with the United States, providing that the federal government would make education available to the Indians.

The Pickering Treaty is signed between the Seneca and the United States.

More Cherokee Indians migrate under pressure, to the Arkansas-Texas area. Cherokee Indians who fought with the English during the American Revolution, now surrender, probably the last to do so of the English forces.

A treaty is signed at Greenville by the Potawatomi, the Kickapoo, and the Commonwealth of Massachusetts. Large tracts of land are ceded to the state.

1799. The "witchcraft" trials of Pueblo medicine men end.

Handsome Lake, Iroquois, makes his prophesies known, and preaches a revision of the old Iroquois religion. A new religious belief springs up around Handsome Lake, which still exists.

Thus ended the 18th century. The Indians were being pushed further and further to the west. The white settlers were taking more and more Indian land. The treaty era began

127

in earnest, between the United States Government and Indian Nations. During this century, forced removal of Indian tribes began, as official actions of the government. In 1786, the United States, in its Confederated Congress, established two departments treating with the Indians: the Northern Department with jurisdiction north of the Ohio River and west of the Hudson River in New York; and the Southern District, which covered the areas south of the Ohio River. A superintendent of each Department reported to the Secretary of War.

In 1787 the Northwest Ordinance was proclaimed, laying the basis for settlement of whites beyond the Allegheny Mountains, and the formulation of early Indian policy under the new government.

When the War Department was created by Congress in 1789, Indian affairs remained a function of the Secretary of War. Congress also, in 1790 passed an Act for the regulation of trade with the Indians.

During this century, and particularly towards its end, it became recognized that the Indians were the critical element in the development of the new United States.

Treaties continued to be made with the Indian Nations until the end of the 19th century, thus recognizing the sovereign status of the tribes, a fact which is not readily recognized today.

During this century, also, a new era of Indian economy began. The horse became a major factor in the native economy, particularly among the tribes of the High Plains.

1800. In the California missions, where Indians are held in forced labor, native deaths are double the births.

Oregon Indians suffer a malaria epidemic which will last for fifty years.

In the early years of this century, the Karankawa Indians fought a desperate battle with Jean Lafitte. A notorious pirate, Lafitte had stolen one of the Karankawa women. They were defeated by superior armaments.

1801. Several Pawnee tribes are decimated by a smallpox epidemic.

1802. The Osage Indians move from Missouri into Oklahoma.

1803. The Kaskaskia Indians cede their Illinois land to the United States Government.

1804. The Sac and Fox Indians are confronted with a treaty which is illegally signed by unauthorized persons, and the Indians lose fifty million acres of land.

1805. The title of the Creek Tribe to their land in the southern part of the country, is extinguished under duress.

1806. Indians of Colorado watch in disbelief as the expedition of Zebulon Pike crosses the Kansas plains and sees (Pike's) Peak for the first time. This gentleman predicted the peak would never be climbed, but Indians had reached the summit many times before. Furthermore, one of his own men climbed it within a month of his prediction.

1807. Joseph Brant, Mohawk leader, dies on November 24.

1809. The Delaware, Potawatomi and other tribes are forced to cede three million acres of their land for seven thousand dollars. Lands included are: Wisconsin, Indiana, Illinois, and portions of Ohio and Michigan.

In this year, under General William Henry Harrison, one of the distinguished American heroes, one hundred million acres of Indian land are ceded to the United States. This was done through threats, bribery, distribution of whiskey, trickery, and intimidation.

1810. On August 12, Tecumseh, a Shawnee leader, repudiates the fraudulent land purchases made in 1809, at a meeting between the Indians and General Harrison's treaty commission.

1811. Tecumseh's brother leads an attack on the Americans, who are led by General Harrison. The Indians are defeated in this premature action at the Battle of Tippecanoe.

The Apache are in rebellion again, following the unsuccessful settlement policy of the United States Government.

The Creek leader, McIntosh, is convicted by his tribe under their "no sale, no exchange" laws. He had signed a false land cession treaty. The sentence was to be carried out fourteen years later.

1814. The Cherokee and Creek Indians, who had supported General Andrew Jackson in the War of 1812, receive a lesson in dishonesty. Jackson turned on his friends in July, demanding and receiving 23 million acres of Creek land, which is nearly all of the state of Alabama and a fifth of the state of Georgia.

1815. The first of many treaties and agreements is signed with the Sioux. A treaty is signed with the Iowa. A treaty is signed with the Potawatomi. All these treaties cede land by force to the United States.

1816. The Comanche and Kiowa are victims of smallpox, which severely decimates their population.

A treaty is made with the Winnebago.

1817. The Delaware cede all their remaining land.

1818. The Quapaw Indians cede all their remaining lands. Reservation land is set aside for them, a mere fraction of their original holdings. A treaty is made with the Osage, giving them parcels of land which have already been ceded to Cherokee who migrated into Arkansas. The treaty with the Tamaroa is made, ceding all their lands in Illinois, and providing for their removal. A treaty of land cession is signed with the Peoria Indians.

The Seminole Indians begin to war against the United States. The Dade battle took place in this year, in which one hundred troops of the United States Army were wiped out by the Indians. This was to continue until the mid-1830's.

1819. The Kickapoo people cede their land to the United States.

1820. The Indians of Maine are dismayed to find, that when the state of Maine is created from the Commonwealth of Massachusetts, the 395,000 acres of land which had been set aside for them, is now sold off, and the proceeds from the sale placed in the state treasury. This involves the Passamaquody Indians.

1821. Sequoya, after twelve years of labor, presents the Cherokee Nation with a syllabary of their language. In less than a year, illiteracy is banished from the Cherokee people by 90 per cent. The nation has a font of type cast, with which they print the laws of their people.

Indians in areas of California, Arizona and New Mexico have new appressors when Mexico declares its independence from Spain. The same system of feudal forced labor continues, but the missions are secularized, and Indians, who have been promised the land of the missions following secularization, are turned out to starve.

1823. The Seminole Indians sign a treaty establishing a reservation. The reservation is almost immediately attacked and raided by whites who are searching for runaway slaves. The Secretary of War has approved the raids.

1824. The Quapaw are forced to cede their land and remove to Oklahoma Territory.

In Connecticut a white girl marries an Indian. She is burned in effigy by the Christian whites.

The Iowa Indians cede all their land to the state of

130

Missouri.

1825. The Creek Indians, being made aware of the fact that McIntosh, their chief, has ceded their land without authorization from the tribe, pass sentence of death against him in 1811. He is shot to death by the Creek military society in this year.

The Indians of the United States come under the jurisdiction of another governmental agency, the Bureau of Indian Affairs. The BIA is established under the Department of War.

The first treaty with the Cheyenne is signed.

The Osage and Kansa Indians are forced to cede all their land in exchange for two small reserves.

Some Indian tribal groups make plans to establish an Indian state in Northern Mexico. They are confronted with Mexican troops sent to force them to pay taxes. They resist.

1825-1842. This is the period of the growth and development of the Choctaw Academy, located in Georgetown, Kentucky. The Indians founded this educational institution to provide their children with training in the ways of the white man.

1827. Banderas, the Yaqui leader, is defeated by the Mexican forces. He is set free, and becomes the tribe's governor. The policy of the Mexican government to assimilate the Yaqui by means of allotment of land, is resisted by the tribe.

The Cherokee Nation adopts a constitution. Shortly thereafter, this historic instrument is nullified by the state of Georgia.

1828. At Santa Inez mission in California, torture is being used to suppress all remaining Indian religious practices. Three Indian men are beaten to death for healing their people by traditional medical and medicine man practices.

In Newfoundland, the last living Beothuk Indian dies. The tribe had been exterminated to the last man, in less than two hundred years, due to the bounties for Indian scalps.

1829. Geronimo (Goyathlay) is born to the Apache.

The Delaware Indians, in final cession of their land in Ohio, are forced to remove to Oklahoma Territory.

The Cherokee Nation organizes the Cherokee Temperance Society at New Echota, Georgia, in order to restrain the major white man's disease of alcoholism.

1830. The first issue of The Cherokee Phoenix is printed in February.

The Cherokee Nation is confronted with gold seekers when gold is discovered on their land near Dahlonega, Georgia. Their removal is assured.

The Cherokee Nation enacts the "Blood Law," which carries the death penalty for the sale or exchange of any Cherokee land.

The Western Cherokee are forced to exchange their land in Arkansas for land in Oklahoma Territory. They had no "Blood Law," and the perpetrators of this fraud go free.

After a long period of negotiations with the United States Government, appearances before Senatorial committees, and lobbying at the capitol to protect their land rights, the Cherokee Nation finally comes before the Supreme Court. Justice Marshall, in a case titled *Worcester v. Georgia*, decides that the Cherokee Nation is sovereign, and not subject to the state or federal forces. President Andrew Jackson violates the decision of the Supreme Court in a historic mockery of democratic justice, and the policy of Indian removal is made effective.

The United States Indian Removal Act is passed by Congress. Eastern Indian tribes are faced with removal.

1831. The Choctaw people are removed to Oklahoma Territory. The Seneca Indians cede some of their land.

The Nat Turner rebellion occurs in Virginia. A major cause of this revolt is that whites are being permitted entrance into Indian land for the purpose of reclaiming Negro slaves who have escaped and found asylum with the Indians.

The Black Hawk War begins.

1832. On May 9 the Seminole are called in to treat with Treaty Commissioner Gadsden. Unauthorized Indians who are designated as "chiefs," sign the illegal treaty in which Florida is ceded to the United States.

Cholera epidemics kill one half of all the Indians in California's Sacremento Valley. Among others, the Shasta people suffer most, losing fully 90 per cent of their population.

The Creem people are forced to cede all their remaining land in the east.

The Black Hawk War is soon over, the Indians being driven through the forests directly into the Bad Axe Massacre on August 3. Abraham Lincoln is a volunteer member of the militia fighting against the Indians in the war.

1833. The Chippewa, Ottawa, and Potawatomi Indians are forced to cede 300,000 acres of their land. They are to be removed.

The Indians in Mexico continue to refuse to accept the policy of assimilation. Their leaders, Banderas and Guttierrez, are executed. Gandara, another leader of the Yaqui people, leads the fighting, which continues through the next ten years.

1834. Bounties are offered for Apache scalps at a price of $100 each.

The Bureau of Indian Affairs is organized within the War Department.

1835. The Comanche Indians make a treaty with the United States, ceding all their Louisiana land. They move to the Brazos river.

The Seminole people receive an ultimatum; remove or be removed by force. Agent Thompson, with his civilian army on their way to force Seminole removal, are ambushed by the Indians at the Battle of the Great Wahoo Swamp. All but three of the troops are killed. This second Seminole war finds 1,500 American troops lost, while only a handful of Seminole Indians are captured. The war cost the government $50,000,000.

Indians face a new threat. Congress enacts the "Reorganization Act," empowering the Army to quarantine Indians for as long as forty years in order to expedite their civilizing process.

The Seminole leader Osceola is captured while under a white flag of truce. He is imprisoned.

The notorious "false treaty of New Echota," is signed by Cherokee traitors.

1836. The Creek Indians are forcibly removed to Oklahoma, losing about one-third of the tribe because of exhaustion, hunger, and physical abuse by the Army.

Congress ratifies the false treaty of New Echota despite protests of the Cherokee Indians. Many liberal Americans in high positions object to the ratification. Dissension over the false treaty arises throughout the United States, threatening to split the Union. Signers of this fraudulent treaty are Major Ridge, John Ridge, and Elias Boudinot. Depredations continue against the Cherokee of Georgia. Rape, murder, and theft is practiced against them, to induce them to remove, and they are finally forced to do so. The cost of removal was deducted from Cherokee funds.

1837. An American citizen named Johnson, who has claimed

to be a friend of the Apache, fires a howitzer into a peaceful camp of the Indians, killing Juan Jose, the Mimbrenos Apache leader, and many more, in order to obtain their scalps for bounty money. Mangas Colorado retaliates, literally emptying New Mexico settlements of whites.

The Kiowa and Apache Indians make a treaty with the United States.

A smallpox epidemic devastates the Mandan Indians, with a toll of 1,500 lives, then spreads to the Hidatsa and Arikara, where the disease wipes out another 2,000 lives. Smallpox then spreads to the Blackfeet, taking 8,000 Blackfeet lives, 400 Sioux, and 2,000 Pawnee.

1838. The Cherokee meet as they are penned into the removal stockades. Their council passes the Oquohee Resolution: all Cherokee laws are to be extended in perpetuity, Cherokee sovereignty is to be recognized in perpetuity, and the New Echota treaty is repudiated. The death penalty is pronounced against those who are responsible for the treaty. The Cherokee Indians, then numbering approximately 18,000, are force-marched to Oklahoma Territory over the *Trail of Tears*. One hundred of the tribe died each day, many from soldiers' bayonets. In all, approximately one-third of the entire tribe died on the way to Oklahoma.

1839. The Cherokee Blood Law is enforced against Major Ridge, John Ridge, and Boudinot, who are executed on June 22 precisely, although separated by many miles in Oklahoma. Such Blood Law deaths continue for some years.

Osceola is assassinated while in a Florida prison. Chief Bowl's Texas Band of Cherokee Indians is annihilated by Texans.

1840. The Winnebago are removed to Oklahoma, losing fully one-half of their people. Most of them return that same year to their own lands, violating instructions to the contrary.

Eastern Cherokee people who remained in North Carolina, going underground, are given a small reservation in that state, in exchange for the lives of the Cherokee martyr Tsali and his sons. In an attempt to save their people, Tsali and his sons have surrendered and give up their lives willingly. They are executed.

1843. Sequoya, the Cherokee linguistic genius, dies.

1844. In Mexico, the Seri and Apache are forced to the warpath, the Mexican authorities sending their armed might against them.

The Cherokee Nation, in Oklahoma, prints its first Oklahoma newspaper, The Cherokee Advocate.

1846. Two million acres of land are ceded to the United States by Kaskaskia Indians. They are allowed to have a small reservation.

1847. The Taos Indians rebel. The Pueblo rebellion is put down by the United States Army.

1849. A cholera epidemic wipes out one-half of the Pawnee and Kiowa Indians.

Col. Washington attacks the Navajo at Two Gray Hills, killing Narbona, one of their leaders.

Gold is discovered in California, beginning a holocaust of death and destruction for the Indians of the region, as well as ecological destruction of the environment.

The Treaty of Guadalupe Hidalgo is signed between the United States and Mexico, and the Indians now have another ruler, the United States.

The Indians of the United States find themselves in the throes of another governing agency, the Bureau of Indian Affairs, which is transferred from the War Department to the Department of the Interior.

1850. The Wintu Indians in California are massacred at Yosemite by whites.

1851. Plains Indian tribes sign the Treaty of Fort Laramie, making land cessions and permitting roads to be built through their land.

1851-52. The United States sends commissioners to make treaties with the Indians in California. Eighteen such treaties (and one agreement) are signed. But the Senate refuses to ratify the treaties. The Indians fulfill their part of the treaty stipulations, the government does not carry out its provisions. The Indians are not informed that the treaties have not been ratified, and their lands lost to them, until 1905.

1852. One hundred Indians are killed near Weaverville, California, in retaliation for the killing of a miner by an Indian in the town. The Indians are ambushed in a gulch, and shot. One surviving young girl is sold in the town for $45.

A treaty is signed by the Mescalero and Chiricahua Apache Indians at Santa Fe, on July 1.

1854. The Oto Tribe cedes its Nebraska land to the United States.

Washington State tribes cede two-thirds of their land at the Treaty of Medicine Creek, reserving certain lands and the right to hunt and fish in perpetuity.

1855. The Sioux-Cheyenne camp on the Blue Water Creek is attacked by General Harney on September 3. Hundreds are killed, and many prisoners are taken. The war being prepared as the result of such actions is to last twenty five years.

The Cheyenne people at Ash Hollow are attacked and massacred.

1857. In this year the Teton Sioux hold a Great Council meeting.

General Sumner's calvalry attacks the Cheyenne.

The Yaqui, led by Gandara and Marquinn, go to war against the Mexican government.

Indians are blamed for a massacre of 120 unarmed settlers instigated and carried out by Utah Mormons. The Massacre of Mountain Meadows goes down in Anglo history as the fault of the Indians. While a few Indians were present, the deed was committed with the knowledge and active participation of the Mormons. Mormon patriarchs and leaders have organized the massacre. Brigham Young had given instructions for the disposal of the $100,000 worth of property, and the division of the captured children. Money from the sale of the property goes to the Mormon church. Orders for the massacre have come from high officials. In later years, when a trial could no longer be avoided, one man was sacrificed for the deed.

1858. The Comanche, returning from a meeting with officials of the United States Government, are attacked by the United States 2nd Cavalry and the Texas Militia.

Indians and Mormons are in conflict over the Mormon attempt to convert the Hopi Indians.

1859. Kansa Indians are forced to cede one half of their reservation to the United States. The Caddo tribes on the Texas Brazos river are forced to move to Oklahoma by the Texans, and are removed to the Washita river.

1860. On February 25, sixty women and children near Eureka are massacred in California. The men were away from home, hunting.

Six thousand Navajo are reported to be in slavery in New Mexico. They attack Fort Defiance, and are defeated.

The Paiute Indians at Pyramid Lake defeat miners who have come to attack them.

1861. On February 18, the Cheyenne and Arapaho make a treaty ceding their lands in Kansas, Wyoming, Nebraska, and Colorado, only excepting the triangular reservation located near the Big Sandy Creek on to the Purgatoire river in southeastern Colorado.

The Apache, at a meeting of truce with the United States, under a white flag, are taken prisoner, Cochise escapes, but Lieut. Bascom kills all the rest.

1862. Indians' lands in the west are opened up to white settlers through the Homestead Act, passed by Congress in this year.

Cochise and Mangas Colorado open up a war of the Apache against the United States.

Reservation Sioux in Minnesota, dependent by this time upon annuities and supplies for a mere living, depend upon the trader's credit. The annuities are late, and the traders refuse further credit. They must hunt before winter, but they dare not leave before their goods arrive. They wait. The traders cut off all their credit. When told the Indians are hungry, Agent Myrick says "Let Them Eat Grass." Tension mounts, and an uprising ensues. Myrick is one of the first to die at the hands of the Indians. He is found with a hunk of prairie grass stuffed in his mouth. In this rebellion, the Sioux literally devastate and clear twenty-three counties of whites. Thirty-eight Sioux are hanged at Mankato, Minnesota.

1863. Little Crow, a Minnesota leader of the Sioux, is killed.

The Wallowa sign away their land in the Treaty of Lapwai.

In Canada, Indian leaders, including Ahcheewun, are hanged for resisting gold prospectors on their land.

The Yuman Indians resist gold prospectors of the Prescott, Airzona, strike.

Eleven years of war begins, in which four hundred Americans and one thousand Havasupai are killed.

The Utes sign a treaty in which they are given a reservation in Colorado, in exchange for most of their land.

Mangas Colorado, Apache, is captured under a white flag of truce. He is tormented, bayoneted, and tortured into trying to escape. He is then shot.

Governor Pesquire of Sonora, Mexico, offers $100 for Apache scalps. Apache children are to be sold as slaves.

The Navajo Nation learns that Kit Carson has been commissioned to subdue them. He destroys all their fruit trees, of which there were about four thousand at this time, then fifteen thousand head of their sheep and cattle. In the winter, Carson besieges them, starving them into submission. Atrocities are committed by Carson's soldiers. The Navajo are then imprisoned for four years, and during this time of captivity more than half of the tribe dies.

The Nez Perce are forced into reservations.

1864. More than three hundred peaceful Cheyenne are attacked by Chivington's Colorado Militia at dawn, on November 28. Atrocities are committed which stirred public protest, ending in an investigation.

1865. The Sioux attack Julesburg. The Platt Bridge battle occurs, in which the Sioux overwhelm United States troops.

In Arizona, the Chiricahua Indians take Fort Buchanon.

1866. On August 1, Chief John Ross of the Cherokee Nation died.

On December 21, Indians meet Captain William Fetterman as he rides out of the fort to attack the Sioux. Fetterman had boasted that he could ride through the whole Sioux Nation if he had but eighty men. He had eighty-four men on this day, fell into an ambush on the Bozeman Trail, and into the arms of a brigade of Sioux, Cheyenne and Arapaho. His men were killed. He and another officer committed suicide. The bugler fought to the last. For his extreme bravery, he was not mutilated, but was found covered with a buffalo robe. The fort was closed, and the Indians had won this battle.

1867. The Sioux fight the Wagon Box battle. The United States Army has repeating rifles by this time, and the Sioux lose some of their finest warriors and nearly five hundred men.

The Cheyenne, Arapaho, Kiowa and Comanche sign the Medicine Lodge Treaty with the United States. Land cessions and removal to Oklahoma are provided for.

The Yaqui in Mexico are disarmed by the government.

Fraud, thievery, and misconduct in the Bureau of Indian Affairs, so long a complaint of the Indian tribes, is finally investigated.

The Natives of Alaska are unaware of the fact that the United States and Russia have signed a treaty in which the United States has purchased the state of Alaska. The treaty provides that citizenship, (and implicitly, land title), be withheld from the "uncivilized natives." This issue is to result in a massive land claim, because of the failure to negotiate with the natives instead of with a foreign power.

1868. The Sioux are forced to sign a new Fort Laramie Treaty, in which the railroads will be permitted to go through their territory. Red Cloud signs the treaty, and is denounced as a traitor.

Custer's First Stand takes place in September, at the battle of the Washita river, in which he loses twenty men. He attacks a peaceful camp, and Black Kettle, Cheyenne chief, is killed.

Roman Nose, Cheyenne, is killed at the battle of Beecher Island.

The imprisoned Navajo Nation is permitted to return to their land.

1869. In Los Angeles, California, Indians are given free booze, so that they may be arrested for drunkenness and sold into slavery on Monday morning.

The Kiowa Indians enter their Oklahoma reservation.

The Utes are forced to make a treaty with Kit Carson, representing the United States Government.

1870. The United States introduces a policy of destruction of Indian religion. The slogan is "destroy the religion and you will destroy the tribal leadership."

Louis Riel leads the Winnepeg-Red River Indians in a war of independence to establish an Indian state. The government, at this time, agrees.

The Tuscarora people are given smallpox-laced blankets after they have removed to Kansas territory.

Captain Jack of the Modoc Tribe attempts to reclaim their land. The Modoc war starts in Oregon.

1871. The Indians learn that the United States, by a devious route, through an enabling Act of the Congress, have ended treaty making with the tribes. However, agreements and executive order decisions remain in treating with the Indian tribes and nations.

Satank, Satanta, and Big Tree of the Kiowa Tribe, are arrested. Within a few years, two have committed suicide, or presumed to have committed suicide during their imprisonment.

The Blackfeet, Assiniboine, and Cree Tribes in Canada and the United States are hit by smallpox.

In Arizona, women and children are massacred at Camp Grant, and outrageous atrocities occur.

1872. The Modoc people, fighting in the Lava beds, resist the Army. At a peace talk, General Canby is slain. The war continues, and one hundred Modoc tribesmen stand off one thousand soldiers. One by one, the Modoc men are caught and killed. The remaining Modoc Indians are sent to Oklahoma. Two thousand non-combatants are given their own lands in Oregon for a reservation.

1873. The Apache at Camp Apache decide to escape. Three of their leaders are being hunted, dead or alive.

The Kansa Tribe is forced to sell all its remaining reservation land, and then removed to Oklahoma.

Canadian Assiniboine Indians are massacred by whites.

The Ute people cede a portion of their Colorado land.

In Mexico the Yaqui and Mayo tribes are covered in the new Sonora Constitution, Article IV: It is intended "to deprive the Yaqui and Mayo tribes of rights to citizenship while they maintain anomolous organizations that they have in their towns and rancherias, but allowing the enjoyment of those rights to individuals of the same tribes who reside in the organized state pueblos." This rule was aimed at the destruction of Indian tribal sovereignty.

An Indian man in Montana caught and saved four buffalo calves. In a few years, after the great buffalo slaughter, his calves would be the only remaining buffalos, and from them would come the herds that exist today.

1874. Pyramid Lake Reservation is created in Nevada by President Grant, by Executive Order.

The Yaqui rebel against the continual pressure of the Mexican Government to assimilate.

The Ute Indians cede a strip of land seventy by one hundred miles in the San Juan mining area of Colorado.

Indians in the Black Hills Sioux territory are again menaced when Custer discovers the lure of gold. He proclaims it to be an extraordinary discovery and the prospectors are again on the march against Indian land and rights.

In Canada, the Red River War begins.

The 4th Cavalry attacks and wipes out an Indian

camp in Palo Duro Canyon.

On June 8, Cochise is slain while unarmed. Other Apache leaders killed in this year are Cochinay, Chuntz, and Chan Deisi.

The Pawnee chief, Pita'leshar, is murdered by whites to rid the tribe of his influence against removal.

Battles occur at Adobe Walls, and the Buffalo Wallow, between Comanches and the United States in Texas. Indians fight against the wanton destruction of the buffalo.

The Apache Tribes, and generally all Arizona tribes, are moved from the War Department jurisdiction, where they had remained these years, to the Bureau of Indian Affairs. President Grant orders the removal of the Apache from the Verde reservation to the San Carlos Reservation.

1875. Apache Tribes are subjected to continued eviction from their reservations to San Carlos. Three bands put up a fight and refuse to move, and are left alone. The Chiricahua are attacked on their own reservation by Mexicans, claiming they had been raiding into Mexico. They are removed to San Carlos and Ojo Caliente. Their leaders, Juh, Nolgee, and Geronimo escape into Sonora. Claiming that raids are being made on Mexican territory, all other Apache are moved to San Carlos, there to be contained. Victorio escapes. He is caught and returned to San Carlos, escaping again and again. The territory which the Apache are accused of "raiding" is their own land, which they refuse to give up.

The Comanche leaders surrender under Quanah Parker, at Fort Sill, Oklahoma, on June 24. The Red River War is over. Only the Apache Indians remain at war on the southwestern plains. They continue to fight for their land.

Instructions from the United States Government constitute an attack against the Indians, primarily concerning the Sioux, Cheyenne, and northern plains allies, and in the southwest, the Apache. The instructions state that all off-reservation Indians are to be considered hostile.

The Sioux are in Lone Tree Council with the United States, which desires to purchase their Black Hills. The council ends with no sale.

Seventy Kiowa Indians are selected to go to prison for depredations. Chief Kicking Bird is assassinated for making this selection under instructions by the whites. The seventy men are sent to a Florida prison.

141

One hundred unarmed Cheyenne are massacred at Sappa Creek on April 8.

1876. The Indians' San Carlos Reservation is overrun by miners. The issue of water rights disputes begins. Geronimo and Victorio, under Chief Nachez, begins open warfare against the United States.

The Ponca people are removed to Oklahoma from Nebraska.

General Miles attacks Crazy Horse camp on the Tongue River in January.

On June 14 the Sioux hold a Sun Dance. Sitting Bull removes one hundred pieces of flesh, and envisions one hundred soldiers falling into the camp. There are nine tribes in this camp, one of the largest ever to be gathered together.

On June 17, the Battle of the Rosebud takes place. General Crook, with 1,500 men, is attacked by at least as many Sioux and Cheyenne with their allies. Crook is forced to retreat, and he is running away all that month, the Sioux in pursuit.

On June 26, Custer attacks the Indian camp. Most of Custer's men are killed or commit suicide. This is known historically as the Battle of the Little Big Horn. Later the Sioux are hunted down, until they are caught and placed on reservations.

On October 21, the Sioux are attacked during a peace council by General Miles.

In December, Sioux men who have come to talk for peace, are killed under a white flag of truce, at Fort Keogh.

1877. Sitting Bull takes his people into Canada.

The Treaty of 1868 is scrapped by the U.S. unilaterally. But the U.S. fails to gain the necessary signatures of three-fourths of the voting males of the tribe.

Geronimo and other Indian leaders are arrested. They escape within a few weeks. Geronimo and thirty-six of his men keep five thousand soldiers busy.

Crazy Horse finally surrenders. The Cheyenne who have surrendered later, are marched for seventy days to Oklahoma.

Chief Joseph's band escapes, eluding and outfighting Army forces. He heads for Canada, a distance of 1,300 miles. Miles short of the Canadian border, he is caught in a brutal crossfire, losing most of his people. He surrenders to stop the slaughter, He and his surviving people are sent to Oklahoma. Crazy Horse is assassinated on September 5.

1878. The Kamia Tribe in Baja California tells of forced baptisms for mission slavery, relating stories of beating, torture, and ill treatment which has lost them one half of their tribe.

In August, the Southern Ute people cede eighteen million acres of their land. Ouray and Sapavanari protest at a land meeting. They want to go to Washington personally to negotiate the sale. They wish to get paid in cash, "since it took years after a sale to collect from the government."

The Cheyenne break out of their Oklahoma Reservation. They have been subjected to hunger and abuse. Corruption of the Bureau of Indian Affairs has deprived them of food and clothing. They head back north to their homeland. They were hunted and killed along the entire route. They continued north, despite the danger and the conditions.

An educational institution is founded in Carlisle, Pennsylvania and is located in an abandoned Army barracks. A new system of education, aimed to train the Indian youth in vocational skills, trades, and manual labor, is instituted by Captain Richard Pratt. The school is run like an Army barracks, but Captain Pratt becomes the darling of many Indian progressives, and his sytem continues for many years after he leaves Carlisle.

1879. In January, sixty-four Cheyenne are killed attempting to escape a temporary prison, which forced starvation upon them. Seventy-eight were recaptured. Dull Knife and Little Wolf, with a handful of Cheyenne, manage to get through to Powder River country in Montana, where a reservation now exists.

The Nez Perce are dying. So too are the Ponca, Papago and Hualapai as a result of the concentration policy. The Cheyenne had fought with sticks against any further attempts to remove them.

In September, the Ute found that their cattle were being stolen, their people were being murdered, and they were being accused of misdeeds unjustly. Their agent, Meeker, had allotted land parcels to them, and then had begun to plow their land for himself. He is forced to stop. Chief Johnson breaks into Meeker's home and beats him up for his continual intrusion into Indian life. Meeker appeals for help from the

United States Army. One hundred cavalrymen are sent. They are forbidden to enter the reservation, but proceed anyhow. The Indians attack, killing Meeker and his family, as well as other non-Indians who are present. One month later, they voluntarily stop fighting. An investigation is begun.

1880. A vigilante force of whites and miners attack the Ute Reservation, killing several Indians.

In January, Juh and Geronimo surrender at White Mountain Agency, with one hundred and eight of their people.

Victorio is killed in Mexico.

The Ponca Reservation has conditions so vile, and the BIA administration is so filled with corruption, that a special investigation is ordered by the President of the United States.

A court decision (Ex Parte Crow Dog) establishes federal jurisdiction on Indian reservations in cases of seven major crimes: murder, rape, burglary, etc.

Indian police forces are formed by the BIA.

In California, the Indian population is counted at a maximum of 18,000 after one hundred and twenty-five years of genocide. Their original population, at the time of Spanish contact, is estimated at one million and not less than 750,000.

1881. A new Apache rebellion is brought about by Mormon encroachments on their lands. The corrupt BIA is accused of unjust treatment, theft, and fraud. Geronimo, Juh, Loco, Nantiatish, Dane, and Nachez leave the reservations. Nockay-Delklinne, a medicine man, is arrested for dancing to revive the dead and to rid the Indian lands of whites. He is convicted and sent to Alcatraz. The leaders, after a battle at Cedar Springs, escape into Mexico.

The Indian religious practice of the Sun Dance is banned by the United States. Plains tribes medicine men are arrested. Religious suppression is rampant.

Sitting Bull returns from Canada and surrenders.

1882. The Hopi Reservation is established in the midst of the Navajo reserve, ostensibly "to protect them from the railroads and the Mormons."

The Apache face further dangers as Mexico and the United States make a treaty permitting troops from either country to pursue Apache beyond the borders.

In Mexico, the Mayo and Yaqui are still at war. Their leaders are periodically captured and shot. A new war has begun, with executions and attempted assassination of Indian leaders by whites.

The Anglo Indian Rights Association is founded, and receives wide publicity through the years. But the Indians themselves, who have formed their own underground organizations and have resisted intrusion on their land as well as on their rights, are ignored.

1883. Apache Indians who are taken prisoner are enslaved in Mexico, continuing a practice lasting more than a hundred years.

An Apache traitor, named "Peaches," aids General Crook in attacking the Apache stronghold in the Sierra Madre. Geronimo, Chato Bonito, Nachez (Cochise's son) surrender, agree to be placed on reservations.

The Kickapoo are removed to Oklahoma. They had taken asylum in Mexico, were attacked by United States troops in Mexico, and were then removed.

1884. The Alaskan Organic Act is passed, and the United States, in a meeting with Alaskan Natives promises "title to Alaskan Native lands."

The Apache leader Kaetena, is arrested for incitement, and sentenced to serve three years on Alcatraz. The pacification program for the Apache under General Crook continues.

1885. The Yaqui and Mayo offer to make peace. The Mexican Government fails to ratify the treaty that has been proposed. The war continues.

The Indian state promised in Canada by that government did not materialize. Louis Riel is asked to lead the Indians again, and war breaks out. The rebellion is put down; Riel and eighteen other leaders are tried, convicted, and hanged. Hundreds of Indians are killed and hundreds more are imprisoned.

The Nez Perce are allowed to return from Oklahoma to the Colville Reservation in the state of Washington.

The Papago Indians fight for a waterhole against the cowboys in Arizona.

The Canadian Indian Act is passed, outlawing Indian cultural and religious practices. The Potlatch feast is forbidden.

Indians are subjected to additional indignities and injustices as the Bureau of Indian Affairs formulates the *Criminal Code*, forbidding the tribes to practice their religions, medicine, and tribal ceremonies. All Indians are subject to imprisonment for breaking the Criminal Code. Students sent to boarding schools are forbidden to speak their language, have their hair cut, and are clothed in uniforms.

In May, resisting the new injustices of the Code, 144 Apache, including Geronimo, Mangus, Nachez, Nana and others break out of the reservation and head for Mexico.

1886. The Mayo and Yaqui in Mexico are devastated by smallpox. The Mexican Army now begins to win some battles, including the Battle of Buatachive, in which 250 Indians are killed and 2,000 are captured. Prisoners are sent into slavery in Yucatan. Both tribes retreat, with their remnants, into the mountains.

In January, Captain Crawford enters Mexico in pursuit of the Apache. His camp is surrounded by Mexican troops, who open fire. The Indians are waiting nearby, watching. They had been prepared to surrender, but move off when the fighting starts.

Some of the Apache surrender at Canyon de los Embudos.

A force of 5,000 Army men under General Nelson Miles moves into Indian country to obtain the final liquidation of the Apache. Many Indians are sent to be imprisoned in Florida. Despite the terms of the surrender, some eleven men are sent separately to Fort Pickens in Florida, and the women and children to Fort Marion. A peace delegation of the Apache goes to Washington to discuss terms and a new reservation. They are told to go home. On September 7 more than 500 Apache are rounded up in Arizona and sent to Fort Marion, Florida, without distinguishing between those who desire peace and those who wish to continue fighting.

1887. The Dawes Act (also known as the Allotment Act) is passed, thus paving the way for breaking up Indian tribal land, making Indian land available to whites, and generally destorying Indian economy and culture. The Act provides that allotments of land be made to heads of families and individuals. At this time the Indians still hold approximately 145,000,000 acres of land, out of a total acreage of land in the United States of 1,950,000,000. After individual allotments are made, 90,000,000 acres are declared "surplus" and taken by the United States to be sold to non-Indians. Rarely were tribes paid for this greatest land grab in American history.

1889. With the Indians in complete ignorance of the plans

of the United States Government, a policy of "termination" is introduced as an active program of elimination and eradication of the Indian tribal structure and life. This was an effort to eliminate tribal land holdings and reservations, individualize the land holdings making them taxable, and to take over as much Indian land into the public domain or into the hands of non-Indians as possible.

Of the 600 or more Apache prisoners in Florida, 140 had died by this date.

On January 1, there is a total eclipse of the sun, during which a Paiute Indian, Wovoka, sees a great vision, in which a ceremony is revealed which will bring back the murdered and dead Indians, and will rid the land of all whites. The *Ghost Dance* religion begins.

1890. The "Keeping of the Soul" sacred death rite of the Sioux Tribes is forbidden by the United States Government.

Religious teachers among the Yaqui and Mayo tell of visions and prophesies, and introduce new religious ceremonies. All work is stopped. Officials arrest the leaders and put them to work in the mines.

The Ghost Dance gains support among the Indians. It spreads into Oklahoma, north among the Sioux, to more than twenty major tribes. The whites surrounding the reservations fear another uprising, and the dances are forbidden. In many cases, the United States sends troops into the dance grounds, and a tense situation becomes one of open hostility. In North Dakota, the respected leader Sitting Bull of the Sioux, is ordered arrested after he refuses to stop the religious ritual of the dances. The orders are to shoot to kill if "any trouble" arises. On December 12 the order is announced, both in English and Lakota. December 15, a group of Indian police attempt to arrest Sitting Bull, and the Indians resist. Sitting Bull is killed. The Indians run to the Badlands, and are pursued by Army troops. Through the Badlands, they escape to Pine Ridge. On December 29, Bigfoot, the leader of the group, suffering from pneumonia, is trapped with three hundred of his people at Wounded Knee Creek on the Pine Ridge Reservation. The troops surround the group. They are remnants of the 7th Cavalry, re-formed after the Custer defeat at the Little Big Horn.

The Indians are disarmed, and take refuge in a gulley. It is said that only one Indian had a gun, but there is little evidence of what transpired then. It is only known that the troops massacre the women and children, and the few men left in the group. They are killed by gattling gun fire, and hacked to death by the soldiers. Only a few escape. The fifteen-year revenge for the defeat of Custer becomes a historic blot on American history.

The Cheyenne-Arapaho lose 3,500,000 acres of their land when the United States sells their land to whites.

1891. Lands of the Kickapoo in Oklahoma are ceded by force, and allotted.

1892. The Kiowa Tribe repudiates the illegal treaty in which their lands were taken.

1893. The Cheyenne Outlet is opened to homesteaders.

The United States, bending to the demands of whites in Oklahoma, who by this time surround most reservations with populations outnumbering the Indians, extinguishes all tribal land titles in the state. This is done preparatory to declaring Oklahoma a state.

Anthropologists at Hopi Reservation steal the sacred ceremonial objects from the kivas. These are exhibited in the Chicago Exposition.

1894. Congress acts to allow the Apache prisoners in Florida to return west. They are sent, with their families, to Fort Sill, Oklahoma.

1896. Indians with their traditional long hair are subjected to personal ridicule and intimidation by the United States through the Bureau of Indian Affairs. Long-haired Indian men have their hair cut at gunpoint.

1897. The Yaqui leader, Tetabiante, surrenders to Colonel Peinado after lengthy negotiations, in which the Yaqui are guaranteed recognition of their tribal sovereignty.

1898. The Dawes Commission is established to prepare rolls of the names of Indian families living on reservations to enable the allotment of their land. Many non-Indians, through fraud, are included on these rolls. Many Indians, through fraud, are excluded from the rolls.

1899. In Mexico, Tetabiante is made head of the recently surrendered Yaqui forces. The promises to observe tribal sovereignty are violated, and the Yaqui are preparing to rebel again. The Mexican-Yaqui war starts again.

A comprehensive treatment of the history of the Indians

of America would take thousands of printed pages. Every year of the 19th Century is filled with history. The keynote of the century was war with the Indians, and an attempt to extinguish their title to the continent, as well as deliberate genocidal actions.

Only a brief overview is given here, of events that shaped the history of this nation and ended in the destruction of a whole race. Remnants remain today, but the grand panorama of a proud and numerous race is gone.

This Chronology takes the reader only to the end of the 19th century. The fifth volume in The American Indian Reader series, dealing with current affairs, will continue the chronology through the 20th century to the present.